The Biographer's Craft

THE

Biographer's
Craft

MILTON LOMASK

PERENNIAL LIBRARY

Harper & Row, Publishers, New York
Cambridge, Philadelphia, San Francisco, Washington
London, Mexico City, São Paulo, Singapore, Sydney

Grateful acknowledgment is made for permission to reprint:

Excerpts from *Testament of Youth* by Vera Brittain. Copyright 1933 by Vera Brittain. Reprinted with permission of the Literary Executors for the Vera Brittain estate, Victor Gollancz Ltd. and the Putnam Publishing Group.

Excerpt from "Lives of the Saints and the Secular" by Peter Prescott from the October 29, 1984, issue of *Newsweek*. Copyright © 1984 by Newsweek, Inc. All rights reserved. Reprinted by permission.

First PERENNIAL LIBRARY edition published 1987.

Library of Congress Cataloging-in-Publication Data
Lomask, Milton.
  The biographer's craft.

  "Perennial Library."
  Bibliography: p.
  Includes index.
  1. Biography (as a literary form) I. Title.
CT21.L58 1987   808'.06692   85-45211
ISBN 0-06-091387-8 (pbk.)

---

87 88 89 90 91 MPC 10 9 8 7 6 5 4 3 2 1

To Randall Metcalf

Contents

Caught up in a technological society, man tends to feel himself increasingly dehumanized; thus he once more reaches for the lives of others to assure himself of the commonalities of existence.

—*Leon Edel*

The Biographer's Craft

CHAPTER *1*

Your Job

SOME years ago Catherine Drinker Bowen, that delight-ful and delighting American biographer, was startled by the "magisterial" assertion of a novelist friend that "compared to fiction writers, biographers have an easy time. Their plot is ready to hand before they even begin to write." When Bowen asked, "What plot?" the novelist said it was obvious: "Birth, education, marriage, career, death."

With six full-length biographies behind her, Bowen real-ized that her friend was talking about "chronology," a form some biographies take but not at all what a biography is.

The writer of "life portraits," to borrow a useful term from Leon Edel, is a bizarre, ambidextrous creature. He works, as Paul Murray Kendall has observed, with a shovel in one hand and a pen in the other: the shovel to acquire the facts he needs, the pen to distill them into what he hopes will be a compelling story.

If the two broad fields of prose—fiction and nonfiction—can be represented by two intersecting triangles, thus · · · ⋊ · · · , then the biographer can be described as operating along the dotted line at the center. Gathering his material, he uses the quasi-scientific methods of the historical researcher; writing his book, he uses the techniques of the fiction writer. Like a short story or a novel, a biography needs a central tension around which the material you assemble can be organized so as to leave in the mind of the reader some dominant impression or statement, some major theme with which the subsidiary themes resonate, to which they contribute even as small streams contribute to the making of a river. A biography is not a compilation of facts. It is a portrait in words of a man or woman in conflict with himself, or with the world around him, or with both.

To suggest that it emulate fiction is not to say it should *be* fiction. What baffles me about the fictionalized lives I've read is why their authors bothered. As Virginia Woolf has remarked, the writing of a life has this in common with the writing of anything: the game's no fun unless you play by the rules. And the rules are clear. Today's lover of biography comes to your table for meat and potatoes, not for papier-mâché. Truth, the old saying goes, makes bad fiction, but fiction should read like truth. Similarly, fiction makes bad biography, but biography should read like fiction.

Can the word "biography" be pinched into a definition? Not comprehensively, and certainly not briefly. There are so many kinds of biographies; the form lends itself to so many different purposes.

There's the narrative biography, in which you carry an individual from cradle to grave, though not necessarily in that order. James Flexner's *George Washington* and W. A. Swanberg's *Citizen Hearst* are examples of it. If you choose as your subject a living person, you carry him to some high point in his life. This sort of work, to be sure, is a profile, a tentative appraisal of your individual as distinct from the full appraisal the word "biography" implies.

There's the topical biography, in which you try to suggest the whole of your subject by splitting it into its parts: Jefferson as a diplomat . . . as a politician . . . as a farmer . . . as an architect . . . as a philosopher and so on; a chapter perhaps to each facet of the man. This subform has proved useful to writers of collective biographies: to Lytton Strachey in his *Eminent Victorians,* to Paul C. Nagel in *Descent from Glory: Four Generations of the John Adams Family.* Edel employs a variant of it in *Bloomsbury: A House of Lions.* Discussing his word-pictures of the nine individuals this biography covers, he describes them as resting on

> an episodic structure and a psychological interpretation of Bloomsbury's past. My episodes are strung together as one strings beads—and when the string is complete and harmonious, each bead has a relation to the other beads. . . . My Bloomsbury personages met in youth; they became friends; they struggled into maturity; they courageously faced the world's turmoil; their lives became intertwined. There are many novels which tell such a story—the story of an *Entwicklung,* an unfolding. To tell it in biographical form, as if it were a novel, and to be loyal to all my materials was the delicate and amusing task I set myself.

There's the "and" biography. In this you concentrate on the relationship of two individuals (Strachey's *Elizabeth and Essex*) or on that of an individual and an institution or group (Swanberg's *Luce and His Empire*) or on an individual as a prism on history (Barbara Tuchman's *Stilwell and the American Experience in China*).

And there's the essay type often spoken of as the portrait: informal, discursive, with the author occasionally stepping outside the frame of the story to comment on it in the simple first-person "I," lingering over the peaks of his hero's life as he writes and brushing over the valleys—a difficult form to bring off, Bowen tells us, but enchanting when well done, as she herself has demonstrated in her *Francis Bacon: The Temper of a Man.*

The subforms mentioned—narrative, topical, "and," and essay—do not begin to exhaust the possibilities. Not only are you free to experiment with form, but it is imperative that you do so—that before embarking on a full writing schedule you weigh with care the several likely ways in which your story can be told. A biography—and this can be said of all writing for the general reader—consists of a what and a how. The what is your subject, along with anything you can learn about it; the how is the template, the pattern in which you cast your portrayal. Any subject can be presented in half a dozen ways. Five of them may give you a satisfactory story, the sixth an excellent one.

Writing a life is a process, during which the author must cope with a variety of problems. Its main steps are well known. You find a subject. Then you do your research. Then you write—and rewrite. As this is the standard sequence, this would seem to be a useful order in which to discuss the techniques, methods, procedures, and principles involved.

CHAPTER *2*

Selecting and Testing a Subject

LIKE Bowen's novelist, I too can be magisterial. "The best subject for a biography," I remember telling one of my writing classes at Catholic University of America, "is not the one you seek, but the one that seeks you."

Subsequent experience has taught me that more misleading words were never spoken.

Personal interest often tells you where to look for someone to write about: the lawyer looks for a brilliant and influential jurist, the student of literature for a great author, the doctor for a medical genius, the lover of the theater for a star of stage or screen. But in the end the idea that promises an effective book almost always turns out to be the one that found you only because you were conscientiously and probably even desperately looking for it.

The hunt for a subject is easily the most crucial of the three big steps by which a biography is produced. "There are no rules for composition," Claude Debussy said, "but every composition makes its own rules." Discovering the rules appropriate to your project, achieving the right organization of your material, the right style, and the right tone: these chores can be a bewildering exercise in trial and error, in writing and rewriting. But by courage and persistence you can overcome all the problems natural to biographical writing—all, that is, except the failure to pick the subject that is right for you.

Seldom can a life be written quickly. Often it takes years, and during this time you find yourself living with another person. While I was gathering material for an account of Aaron Burr, friends chided me for choosing as my literary roommate a man whose claims to fame were that he killed Alexander Hamilton in a duel, got himself tried for treason, and mounted a lugubrious and probably illegal adventure called the "Burr Conspiracy." My defense: Burr was daring, reckless, brilliant, amusing, exasperating, and outrageous—in short, good company.

Self-knowledge is the most reliable guide for making your selection. The best subject is a person whose likes and dislikes, interests, attitudes, background, and dreams are roughly consonant with your own. Sinner or saint, it matters not, so long as you find the individual engrossing. "It is impossible," Doris Kearns has said, "to write a book about a bore without becoming boring."

However the idea for your subject comes to you—out of the blue (a rare blessing) or only after you've eliminated all but one of a long list of possibilities—it is not a good idea to plunge at once into research. Stop—before you start. Think awhile. Brood awhile. At this stage of the game I buy a nice clean notebook. At the top of the first page I place the name of the subject I'm considering. Then, pen in hand, I start chatting with myself about it. In time this workbook becomes a biography of the biography.

"But how can I do what you suggest?" you ask. "I've done no systematic research. I don't know enough yet to talk about the topic."

You know more than you think; you've done some reading on the subject or you wouldn't be considering it: in encyclopedias perhaps, in biographical dictionaries, in newspapers or magazines. Are there already one or more biographies of your hero? Read them.

Read between the lines. In the best of these books you

notice that the mother of your hero—Ed, we'll call him—is often mentioned, but nowhere in the biography is there so much as a sentence about the nature of their relationship. Maybe the author could find no information on that. Scribble a note to yourself: "See if there's any material around on how Ed and his mother got along."

Go further. Using the little you know about mother and son, write a description of how they affected one another. Make it up. But that's fiction, you protest. There should be no fiction in a biography. Of course not. But you're not writing the book now, you're simply testing a subject. Like a muscle, the imagination strengthens with use, and there's no reason why you shouldn't take advantage of this testing period—this period of relative ignorance—to limber yours up. When you begin real research, you'll be glad you did. For only with the help of your imagination can you develop what is probably the most useful capacity a researcher can have—the ability to spot the relationships between facts that at first glance appear to have no connections whatsoever. "Write your treatise first," I've heard historians advise, "and then take your notes."

Fill your workbook with questions: any questions about the subject, no matter how trivial, that occur to you. The question is the teller of lives' most important tool. Difficult as it may be to say in a few words what a biography is, the writing of one can be defined as a struggle to answer all the questions that the accessible material provokes. The job of the biographer is to uncover and convey the unobvious truth.

Tough questions are the best. Joseph P. Lash, in the introduction to his *Love, Eleanor,* describes the shock he suffered one afternoon when at the Franklin D. Roosevelt Library, where he was doing his research, he came upon some "clearly anti-Semitic" letters that his subject, Eleanor Roosevelt, had written during the First World War. The documents now before him were at odds with his perception of Mrs. Roosevelt as a woman of compassionate broad-mindedness. Lash shoved the offending letters to a corner of his desk and left the library, hoping that "somehow . . . overnight" they would disappear. But on his return the next morning they were still there and he knew that he was going to have to deal with them.

"It has been my experience," he comments, "that it is precisely the unsettling document of this kind, the material or interview . . . that upsets preconceptions, that is most productive. It prods the biographer away from shallowness and conventionality. It gives his portrait depth and density and enables him to invest it with some of the complexities and ambiguities which, if we look at ourselves, we see present in our own natures."

Suppose that your hero is the Chief Justice of the United States who in the early years of the nineteenth century took issue with a powerful President to establish the principle that the judiciary branch of the federal government can nullify laws inconsistent with the tenor of the United States Constitution. Even the threat of removal from office by impeachment failed to deter him, and you have come to regard your hero fondly as a fearless battler for the right.

Then suddenly, thanks to a few previously overlooked sentences, you encounter a jolting discovery. On one occasion the Chief Justice actually took fright, going so far as to advocate that the Constitution be amended to permit the members of the national legislature to review and disallow Supreme Court decisions!

What are you to make of this revelation? You can't ignore it. To do so would be to destroy the reality for which you are striving. You can only wonder why. Why this one time did your hero display the white feather? Was he alarmed at the prospect of losing his job? If so, for what reasons? What was his financial condition at the time? Was he perhaps deeply in debt? Was someone he loved ill and in need of expensive medical attention?

You've already read your eyes out, gathering facts about

this man. Now, you realize wearily, you must read further and gather more.

What you are doing in this brooding phase of the writing process is feeling for your subject, getting the excitement of someone else's life into the pores of your skin so that you can share it with readers. "If you would make me cry," the Roman poet Horace said, "you must first cry yourself."

You know from the prologue of *Zelda,* a biography of the wife of F. Scott Fitzgerald, that its author, Nancy Milford, felt her way into her subject long before she began work on it. "When I was young in the Midwest," she writes:

> . . . it seemed to me a fine thing to live as the Fitzgeralds had. . . . Together they personified the immense lure of the East, of young fame, of dissolution and early death—their sepia-tinted photographs in rotogravure sections across the country; Scott, in an immaculate Norfolk jacket . . . Zelda brightly at his side, her clean wild hair brushed back from her face. But it was not her beauty that was arresting. It was her style, a sort of insolence toward life, her total lack of caution, her fearless and abundant pride. If the Fitzgeralds were ghostly figures out of an era that was gone, they had nevertheless made an impact on the American imagination that reverberated into my own generation. I wanted to know why.

One deduces from Milford's words that when she settled into the writing of her book she was buoyed by a sense of purpose, by a desire to say something of consequence about Zelda Fitzgerald. Interesting as Aaron Burr was as the Peck's Bad Boy of American history, I would have hesitated about doing a book on him had not earlier biographies convinced me that Woodrow Wilson was right when, standing at Burr's grave in Princeton, New Jersey, one evening, he murmured to himself, "So maligned, so misunderstood." Who could pass up an opportunity to try his hand at the ticklish business of salvaging a tarnished reputation?

Another thing to be kept in mind during the testing-of-the-subject phase is the matter of residue. "Tell me," I said recently to a lawyer friend, "would you be interested in reading a biography of Franklin D. Roosevelt's engaging campaign manager and Postmaster General, Jim Farley?" The lawyer shook his head. "Too contemporary," he said. "No residue."

Most likely that was the matter Nancy Milford had in mind when she noted that although the Fitzgeralds belonged to "an era that was gone," they had "made an impact on the American imagination that reverberated into my own generation." The residue the Fitzgeralds left behind made them worthy of biographical attention.

When you find that the subject under scrutiny is indeed yours, that you have strong feelings about it, are you ready to start the research and writing?

The answer depends on the level of your experience. I am speaking now of the grim facts of publishing in today's world. Pertinent to this problem is a pleasant memory I have of a night many years ago when the accomplished mystery writer Rex Stout agreed to talk to a writing class I was then conducting at New York University. "When you've finished a piece and figure you've done the best you can with it," he told the students, "package it up and send it off. Who knows? Some damn-fool editor may buy it."

Good advice for fiction writers, but for life writers I'm not so sure. "Fiction," Hemingway said, "is invention from whatever knowledge you have." Because the storyteller writes out of his head, his every piece is or should be *sui generis.* But as a teller of lives you draw your sustenance from a common stock of knowledge that is open to all. If you've published one or more biographies and they were well received, some editor may indeed welcome anything you offer. But if you're doing your first such book, or if previous efforts

enjoyed only moderate success, refrain from committing yourself to any idea, however congenial, until you have evaluated
it in the light of a couple of practical considerations:

What books on this subject are in print? "In print," of
course, means in stock. A book remains in print as long as the
publisher has copies for sale. When the stock goes and the
publisher decides to issue no further copies, the book becomes
"o.p.," meaning out of print.

To determine what's in print on your topic, look it up in
the latest issue of a reference work available in most libraries:
Subject Guide to Books in Print. In addition, check the library
catalog. If, subsequent to the publication of the *Subject Guide*
you're using, another book on your idea has appeared, the
catalog may show it; and you can double-check the library
index by scanning the lists of upcoming publications in those
issues of the trade magazine *Publishers Weekly* that have come
out during the lifetime of the current *Subject Guide.*

Record whatever items you find and their publication
dates. Now you know what your competition is. If a book
similar to the one you're planning has been published within
the last five years, you may want to think twice before continuing with a project that skittish editors may reject on the
grounds that the market is "crowded." If you do proceed, the
editor to whom you send the manuscript will expect you to list
what books on the subject are in print. Be prepared to synop-
size their contents for him, and to do this in a way which
indicates that the work you are submitting has something fresh
and significant to say. Helpful in drafting such synopses is
another reference tool found in most libraries: *Book Review
Digest.* Using the issues of this work covering the year (or the
year after) each of the titles on your list was published, look
them up by author. The extracts from the reviews of the books
will assist you in deciding which of them to read and summarize.

What unpublished subject matter is available? Lytton Strachey, whose still widely read biographies appeared in the early decades of the present century, "worked almost entirely from published sources which he re-fashioned aesthetically and reinterpreted." It is a commentary on how standards have advanced since Strachey's day to learn from Michael Holroyd that for his 1967–68 biography of Strachey he inspected "over thirty thousand letters from, to, and about my subject, in addition to trunks full of miscellaneous papers, diaries, speeches, autobiographical pieces, poems and so on."

For a major biography, you are going to need as much of the kind of material Holroyd mentions as you can find. It's amazing sometimes the sidelights on a person that a laundry slip, a checkbook, a shopping list—any scrap of paper on which your hero scribbled—can provide. Even if no writing adorns these bits and pieces, the knowledge that your person handled and used them makes them part of the unpublished subject matter your work is almost certain to require.

How you go about locating material of this sort depends on the nature of the subject. It was Duke Ellington who put the question: "Biographies, like statues, are for dead men, aren't they?" Not necessarily. Some writers prefer to deal with living individuals. When writing about such people, the obvious procedure is to get in touch with your subject by way of ascertaining what papers he has and to what extent he will let you examine them. If he says nothing doing, try some of his associates, friends and foes alike: people who may have commented on him in diaries and journals, or be in possession of correspondence with or about him.

If there are biographies on your subject, in or out of print, scan their bibliographies and jot down the identifying labels and repositories of the unpublished matter their authors consulted. At this point perhaps a little voice at the back of your head will whisper that there's more. A teller of lives learns quickly to heed this voice; it's probably your unconscious speaking. Try the nearest library with a strong reference collection. What you are seeking are finding aids that can point you to unpublished material around the world, to bibliographic tools on the order of *American Book Prices Current, National Union Catalog of Manuscript Collections,* and *Book Auction Records: General Index.* If your library lacks these or similar volumes, never mind. They or photocopies of all or parts of them can be obtained from other libraries by means to be discussed in the next chapter. If your hero has been the object of an inquiry by the federal government, find out from the FOIA officer at the appropriate agency, usually the Department of Justice, what procedures you should follow to obtain the relevant documents by invoking the Freedom of Information Act (FOIA). What you will then request is that an "All-reference" search be made of government files relative to your subject.

So long as you are simply investigating the possibilities of a topic, neither the value nor the reliability of unpublished data need concern you. Those worries can be postponed until you begin serious research. At this preliminary stage of the work, all you need is an awareness of the extent and whereabouts of such material.

Selecting a good subject may be half the battle, but victory is to the biographer who can lay his hands on good subject matter: on information sufficiently ample, rich, and authentic to permit the writer to say something provocative about the human being he has chosen to delineate.

A story is told of Thaddeus Stevens of Pennsylvania, who for some years during and after the Civil War was the most powerful man in the United States House of Representatives. Entering the chamber one afternoon, Old Thad was accosted by an agitated neophyte, who reminded him that the election of a Speaker was at hand and who complained that he didn't know how to vote because both candidates were "rascals."

"Very likely," said Old Thad, "but the question is: which of them is *our* rascal?"

Once you've found your rascal—a decision tantamount to the conviction that you can now find something vital to say about him or her—the next step, a case of doing what comes naturally, is research.

CHAPTER 3

Research: Tools and Mechanics

RESEARCH for a biography is an extended process of asking questions.

You ask questions of yourself. What do you need to know to bring this subject alive on the printed page? Where are the papers? Are any descendants of your person around, people who might own documents about their ancestor, or be willing to repeat the traditions about him or her that have been handed down in the family?

You ask questions of libraries, archives, historical societies, museums, art galleries, and print collections. Of books, articles, manuscripts, newspapers, doctoral theses (wonderful for facts not readily obtainable elsewhere), oral histories, movies, and recordings. Who would dream of doing a life of William Jennings Bryan, a spellbinding orator, without trying to track down recordings of the great man speaking? He who would write feelingly of Mozart must listen to Mozart.

Right from the start you know that you can't catch your hero simply by confining your search to what he did and said and thought. You must read all around him, poke into every niche and cranny of his life and times. You've elected to write of Ephraim McDowell, a Kentucky surgeon who in the opening decades of the nineteenth century won acclaim as an "artist of the scalpel" because of his skill at removing stone from the human gallbladder. You know that sooner or later you're going to be reading tomes carrying such forbidding titles as *Diseases of the Gallbladder and Allied Structure.*

You ask questions of places. Small wonder that as you read Samuel Eliot Morison's *Admiral of the Ocean Sea* you feel at times as though you were out there in the heaving wastes of the ocean on one of those frangible seagoing tubs commanded by his hero, Christopher Columbus. As part of his preparation for that book, Morison journeyed by sloop, government patrol boat, and barkentine across the Atlantic, following his subject's course and using fifteenth-century methods of navigation in an effort to duplicate Columbus's experiences.

If you can't travel, read. Marchette Chute, gathering data for her *Shakespeare of London,* did ninety-nine percent of her research at the New York Public Library. Seeking to reconstruct the conditions under which Shakespeare labored as a playwright and actor, she read only contemporary documents, such as the parish and corporation records of Elizabethan London. Shortly after her book appeared, Chute took her first trip to the British capital, writing later that on her arrival there she felt as if she had come "back home."

You ask questions of people. You do this not only by interviewing those who have the knowledge you require, but also by training yourself to be observant. Your subject may have been dead for a thousand years, but all people in all ages have much in common. You can learn a great deal about your long-gone hero or heroine by a sensitive study of your own times and the people around you.

One day, in an art store in New York's Greenwich Village, my eye fell on a card tacked to the bulletin board by an art teacher soliciting students. "I cannot teach you to draw," it said, "but I can teach you to see." Like the writer of fiction, the teller of lives should be a good see-er, to say nothing of a good listener.

Harken again to a bit of counsel from Joseph Lash, courtesy of another gifted teller of lives. When Lash set out to write biography, he asked Leon Edel for a few pointers. "Set the scene, Joe," he quotes Edel as telling him. Lash had occasion to remember that advice when he started work on his studies of Eleanor Roosevelt. While Mrs. Roosevelt was alive, he recalls, "I kept diaries. Through her friendship I was privileged to be present at dinners at the White House at which President Roosevelt was often present. The . . . political discussions fascinated me; what I did not note was the setting, the clothes people wore, the motion of the arm and fingers, the pitch of the voice, the glint or glow of the eye, those thousand and one details that enable one to draw a portrait rather than a cartoon."

You even ask questions of your answers. The information you collect is the raw material of your book, similar in function to the clay from which the sculptor shapes his figure. As such, it must be subjected to the refining mind of the researcher, a process so central to the making of a biography that I shall return to it in the next chapter.

When years ago I devised a way of taking notes and storing them so that the information was accessible when the writing began, I thought I had invented something new. Now I know that many writers follow a procedure similar to mine.

For a biography of George Washington, Rupert Hughes used a variant of my system that he called "the butcher-paper method of taking notes." He wrote his notes on a roll of butcher paper, indicating at the left of each entry the category under which it was to be filed and the source or sources from whence it came. When the time came to write, he cut the notes up with a big shears and tacked them under their categories on the walls of his study. I use slugs—names—to identify the categories. Hughes used Roman numerals and remembered what they stood for.

"It was something to watch Father at work," his son, Rush Hughes, has told me. "For his life of Washington, Category I probably stood for Youth, V perhaps for Revolutionary War Career, XV for Presidency, and so on. Father scribbled at a big desk in the middle of the room. Every now and then he'd jump up and trot to this or that wall to examine the notes under I or V or XV or what have you."

That's one way of doing it. Barbara Tuchman tells us that she puts her notes on 4-by-6-inch index cards. She uses these small cards because they force her "to extract the strictly relevant . . . to pass the material through the grinder" of her mind and thus distill it for the potential reader. One reason Tuchman likes this method is that when she travels she can file the cards for the chapter she's working on in a shoebox, or stash the cards in her purse, and go right on writing.

I don't travel much. Besides, I write too large for index cards. I cut 8½-by-11-inch sheets of paper in two, inscribe my notes on these, and file them in manila folders, putting on each folder the name (the slug) of the category of information it is meant to hold. (Users of word processors might wish to type their notes into memory devices, thus eliminating the bother of folders, shoeboxes, and wallpaper.)

While doing my preliminary reading, getting a "bird's-eye view" of the subject, I set up only three folders. One I slug "Sources," another "Q," and the third "X." To explain how these are used, I'll describe the procedure followed when I began work on a life of Aaron Burr. The first book I read was a two-volume biography published more than a hundred years ago. Before dipping into this, I drafted a source card and dropped it into the Sources folder. I headed this card with the last name of the author, followed by the first important word of his title, thus providing myself with a convenient way of referring to the book in the fact notes to be written later. Under this heading I jotted down the im-

print as given in the front of the book along with some information for my own use: a call number for getting the book
at the library and a reminder that I had another edition of
this work on my own bookshelves. That source card looked
like this:

Parton—Life

———, James. *The Life and Times of Aaron Burr.* 2d edn.,
2 vols. NY: Mason Bros., 1964

E202.6.B9P28

Mine is 1-vol reprint of the 1857 edn. No notes or
bibliography in it.

Naturally, source cards for manuscript collections, magazine
articles, interviews with people, letters to the author, etc., had
to be handled differently. One such card read:

Kline—MPAB

———, Mary-Jo et al., eds. Microfilm Edition of the
Papers of Aaron Burr, 1756–1836.

LC and Georgetown Lib. have this. Printed guide to
it on my bookshelf.

Another source card read:

Reubens—Burr

———, Beatrice G. "Burr, Hamilton and the Manhattan
Company," *Pol. Sci. Quar.,* LXXII (Dec. 1957).
LXXIII (March 1958).

H1.P1

Xerox of this in my "Manhattan" folder.

Turning now to the Q folder: while I was doing the preliminary reading and later while doing the real research, sundry questions about Burr arose. As a biography is an attempt to answer all the questions raised by research, I put each of these questions on a card and dropped it into the Q folder. One of the cards:

Q

Why, during the spec. sessn. of the NY leg in Nov. 1800, did AB permit arch-enemy DeWitt Clinton to be elected to powerful Council of Appointment?

At intervals during the writing of the book I glanced through the Q notes by way of making sure that I was picking up the information needed to make the subject and his times understandable to readers.

As for the X folder: while I was doing research on Burr, numerous ways of phrasing portions of the text came to mind—felicitous expressions, possible chapter openings, transitions from one development to another, and the like. Whenever an idea of this sort occurred, I put it on a card and chucked it into the X folder. One contained these huffings and puffings:

X

He had aspired to forge an empire. The failure was bitter, too bitter to be admitted. He had to go on as if his goal were still reachable. To go any other way was to go down into oblivion, into the boredom he had spent his life avoiding. For it was all a game to Burr. He never grew up. He dared not, for to grow up was to face the interior emptiness that is the lot of the unprincipled and the uncommitted.

Just before I started to write, I went through this X folder. By that time I knew more about Burr, and most of the cards sounded silly and overblown. Nonetheless, they helped to get the juices running and made the actual composition easier.

During the serious research I gradually set up the other folders. It took about twenty-five to cover Burr's life and times. Some of the slugs on them read:

"Pre-collegiate." Into this folder went all the information I could find on Burr's life from his birth to his matriculation at what is now Princeton University.

"Soldier." Military career.

"Places." Areas, arranged alphabetically, where Burr lingered, with a separate folder slugged "Places—Richmond."

"Trials." Notes and photocopies on the various grand-jury hearings Burr underwent, with a separate folder slugged "Trials—Richmond."

"People." Notes, arranged alphabetically, on the individuals who figured in Burr's life, with separate folders on his first wife, his daughter, his first wife's family, his own family, his second wife, Thomas Jefferson, General James Wilkinson, and Alexander Hamilton.

"Conspiracy." This development required several folders bearing slugs such as "Conspiracy—Chron" (a day-by-day chronology of the event) and "Conspiracy—Background" (mostly photocopies of articles such as Isaac Joslin Cox's "The Burr Conspiracy in Indiana").

"Amours and Illegitimates." A big folder!

While doing the reading, I used the folders in this fashion. Let's say that on page 32 of the first volume of Parton—Life I came upon information about Burr's childhood. For this I put into the "Pre-collegiate" folder a note reading:

Pre-collegiate
Parton—Life I

32) In his latr yrs AB fond of telling people that
at 4 he ran away from home and stayed "away four days"!
A likely story!

Let's say that on pages 111 and 132 of the second volume of
Parton—Life I found some of Burr's ideas on conducting his
business. In the folder slugged "Lawyer" went a card reading:

Lawyer—things AB told his clerks

Parton—Life II

111) "Now move slowly. Never negotiate in a
hurry."

132) AB called saying "Never put off until tomorrow
what you can do today" "a maxim for sluggards."
Told clerks "never do today what you can do as well
tomorrow, because something may occur that will make
you regret your premature action."

Some writers put one fact only on a card. I crowd in as many
as the card will hold, usually confining myself to material from
a single source. Sometimes, by way of bringing together
things that belong together, I put facts from one source at the
top of the card and related facts from another at the bottom.
That gives this kind of note:

Places (Richmond)—courtrm where AB tried

Personal observation
Room 86' e to w, over 40' wide; deep balconies
reachable by u-shaped stairways at inner corners.

Parton—Life II

48) in AB's day hall doors had iron knob
big enough for a person to sit on
52) "bare" "dingy" "dirty" in those days. Sand-
filled floor boxes for tobacco juice. Not
enough to catch it all

In common with all researchers, when I come across a thought unusually well expressed, I jot it down verbatim on the possibility that I'll want to quote the author. To avoid presenting such phrases or sentences as my own, I set them off in some way on the note card, usually by putting them inside quotation marks; and if I use them thus in the manuscript, I make certain that the reader knows from whom they came. No one needs to be told the reason for these precautions. To palm off other people's phrases or sentences as your own is plagiarism.

It's worth adding that taking notes verbatim should be kept to a minimum. It's easier to copy stuff than to summarize it, and all of us do so far too much, especially when we're in a hurry. Good note-taking is précis writing. The most useful sort of note is a highly condensed paraphrase of the information. Gathering the facts is only a means to an end. Your objective is not to show what a good file clerk you are or even what a good grubber-up of facts. Your objective is to write a book! The sooner you start putting the material into your own words, the better.

Tuchman writes that she uses material from primary sources only. "My feeling about secondary sources," she says, "is that they are helpful but pernicious." She uses them only "as guides at the start of a project to find out the general scheme of what happened." As every researcher knows, "primary" refers to material generated during the lifetime of the subject (diaries, letters, financial records, government files, etc.); "secondary" to works written out of such stuff. Tuchman takes no notes from secondary sources "because I do not want to end up simply rewriting someone else's book." An author, she believes, should never surrender the privilege of selecting from the information those elements that he himself wishes to incorporate in his book. In Tuchman's eyes, one of the things that make a secondary source "pernicious" is that the facts in it have been "pre-selected, so that in using them, one misses the opportunity of selecting one's own."

To this can be added the objection that the facts in a secondary source are pre-digested. They come to you with bits and pieces of another person's opinions and judgments clinging to them. Valid as these may be, they are not *your* opinions and judgments.

Certain it is that you'll produce a fresher biography if for the main line of the story—what your hero did and said, thought and felt—you rely on primary sources. But for the peripheral elements—places where the hero lived and his social, cultural, and political milieu—you may have to turn to good secondary sources. If you confine yourself to primary matter for every word, you may find it impossible to complete the book in a normal lifetime.

As an occasional speaker on biographical writing, I've noticed that when the matter of research arises, different audiences ask the same questions:

Is there a preferable way of taking and storing notes? Perish the thought! Our temperaments and our work habits are too diverse. I've described the system I use for purposes of example only. I can say but one thing for it: it works for me. In actual practice, I ring many changes on it. For example: when I find that I'm getting a vast amount of material from a single source, say a diary or a collection of manuscripts, I make little or no effort to distribute the information among the fact-category folders. Instead I put most if not all of it in a folder of its own. To help me describe the trial of Aaron Burr for treason, I pulled two folders from the file. One was slugged "Trial—Richmond," the other "RG 21, NA," my short title for "Photostatic Copies of Documents in the Aaron Burr Treason Case at the United States District Court of the Eastern District of Virginia, Marion Johnson, compiler, NNGJ, 11 Aug. 1960, Record Group 21, National Archives."

To the many ways of gathering material, only two iron-clad precepts apply: do concoct some sort of system for yourself; and when you have one, use it for everything you write. This is the mechanical aspect of your work. Through repeated use, it becomes automatic, requiring no more attention than does the operation of the keyboard after you've mastered the touch system of typing.

What sort of tools for finding material are available in libraries? Hundreds! If you've not already done so, spend a little time with that best-of-all-possible-friends of the bewildered researcher: *Guide to Reference Books.* A study of the latest edition of this work will save you many wrong turnings, hours of fruitless hunting. From the pages of the *Guide* you will learn, among other things:

That the *Dictionary of American Biography (DAB)* and *Notable American Women (NAW)* cover only dead persons;

that for information about the living you must turn to other tools, such as *Current Biography,* the current volumes of *National Cyclopedia of American Biography, Who's Who in America* and its regional subsidiaries, and *Biography Index;*

that other countries have biographical aids similar to *DAB, NAW,* the various Who's Whos, *Current Biography,* and *Biography Index;*

that when you find your subject associating with persons so obscure no standard biographical dictionary mentions them, you often can track down data on them through the *American Genealogical Index* or a similar aid;

that fruitful sources for people to write about are the American and English versions of *Who Was Who;*

that it's amazing how much information you can trace through *Writings on American History* and *Writings on British History;*

that when your home library does not have an item you want, your librarian has on hand good tools for determining the location of the nearest library that does, and for obtaining the item by interlibrary loan;

that to initiate an interlibrary loan you should give the librarian full information about the item—in the case of a book: author, title, and year of publication at the very least; of an article: author (if any), title, volume of the periodical in which it appeared, and page numbers; of a microfilm: the official title and the number of the reel needed—bearing in mind that the librarian can best help those who help themselves.

Should you do all your research first, or should you start writing while the hunt is still on? If my answer sounds more like a warning against the dangers of procrastination than a reasoned discussion, so be it.

Irrespective of where your research stands, start the writing the minute some of the material begins coming together in your mind. I find it useful to start whenever I glimpse what may or may not become the main theme of the book. At which point I type "Chapter 1" and get going.

To violate a basic rule of writing—namely, say it once and shut up—I repeat what was said above. You are not gathering material to show what a good file clerk and fact-grubber you are. Your objective is to produce a book. Think of research and writing as but the two sides of the same coin. By doing them together, each contributes to the other. Your research gives you something to write about. Your writing alerts you to gaps in your knowledge, to questions for which you have not yet found satisfactory answers.

Get the words down. You can always change them. Indeed, alas, you always will—time and time again. Research can be fun, writing is always hard and time-consuming. A good procedure at the start is to do a lot of research and some writing. A good procedure, as you move along, is to stop for considerably more research as you begin each new chapter— meanwhile gradually decreasing your time at the library and increasing your time at the typewriter.

The point has been well made long since. A writer is not a note-taker. A writer, said Alexander Woollcott, is a person who writes.

NATIONAL PORTRAIT GALLERY MUSEUM SHOP

      10 CASH-1   7197 0008 801

1884873   MDS 1N   1.00
LONGFELLO
1884899   MDS 1N   1.00
HAWTHORNE
1830926   MDS 1N   1.00
BIOGRAPHE
                TOTAL   3.00

   CASH TENDER   3.00
THANK YOU PLEASE VISIT OUR OTHER SHOPS

                    5/03/93 12:53

CHAPTER 4

Research: The Biographer as Detective

W HAT a surprise, lately, to find in the bookstores a tale of espionage with Virginia Woolf, of all people, as the detective. A not uninteresting tale: half the fun lay in watching a gifted novelist, personally fragile and emotionally vulnerable, acquiring the skills and the mind-set of a Sherlock Holmes; half in observing the similarity of those skills and that mind-set to the procedures and attitudes that a biographer must bring to the gathering of the facts.

Ever since my first reading of *The Historian as Detective* (Robin W. Winks, editor), a recounting by twenty-eight historians of their hunt for clues to elusive evidence—to forgeries and misleading documents, to contradictory happenings, straying papers, lost relics, mysterious ailments, and unsolved murders—I have found it consoling, during the drudgery of research, to think of myself as walking in the footsteps of Ross MacDonald's Lew Archer, Rex Stout's Nero Wolfe, and Agatha Christie's Hercule Poirot.

You need a conceit of this sort to keep yourself going when the going gets rough: when the subject's odd behavior forces you to unearth additional data in an effort to understand him; when an undated letter puts you to the labor of determining whether it was written before or after the subject's election to Congress; when a handwritten document is so illegible that you are left wondering whether the papers you're seeking

have been "buried" or "burned"; when again you must identify an individual of Stygian obscurity; when again you must
go far afield in a search for sources if you are to penetrate the
arcana of the subject's profession or philosophy, or to reprise
the aura of his time and place.

The information you need comes from a variety of
sources: from the written word, meaning chiefly manuscripts,
books, and articles; from the spoken word, obtainable by interview or from tapes and records; from graphics, such as
maps, illustrations, and films; from models of places, fauna,
flora, and things; from works of art, such as paintings, sculp-
ture, music, coins, and medals; from personal observation,
usually as an adjunct of travel; and from artifacts—archeologi-
cal findings, for example, or the wedding dress worn by the
heroine.

In *The Modern Researcher,* Jacques Barzun and Henry F.
Graff warn us that none of the items extracted from these
wellsprings of fact and fancy can be used in the form in which
we find them. All must be worked over by the mind of the
researcher. And this working over—this evaluating and veri-
fying of the evidence—constitutes one of the more challeng-
ing processes by which a biography is constructed. Important
to it are certain personal attributes—imagination for one,
skepticism for another, and a capacity for balanced appraisal
for still another.

My college instructors said that to write anything of consequence one must learn to be objective. The human memory
being a porous vessel, it is possible that what they actually
suggested was that one *try* to be objective—good sense, certainly, as distinct from the counsel of perfection implicit in the
admonition to *be* that way. Whatever they said, I left the
university under the impression that objectivity was the alpha
and omega of good writing—a conviction that died fast when
I myself began writing on a professional level.

"Prejudices are the props of civilization"—so André

Gide remarked—and each of us during this earthly pilgrimage acquires his quota. For the biographer, obliged to deal impartially with a subject, the question is this: as you assemble and sift the material, what do you do about your own biases? The answer would seem to be this: the damage that ingrained attitudes can do to your perception of the evidence diminishes in direct proportion to your awareness of them.

As a goal, objectivity belongs in the biographer's tool kit, but so does the realization that it is beyond human grasp. What can be grasped is integrity. As you select and assess the evidence, you can try to compensate for whatever biases you recognize within yourself. As you write, you can be forthright, presenting as facts only those statements you know to be unarguably true, and as opinion those conclusions that you derive from the facts.

Many are the pitfalls awaiting the biographer-as-detective. One of the deepest of them is the tendency common to all of us to become so emotionally involved with our heroes and heroines that we become them.

Edel speaks of this process as "transference." Reminding us that this term is used "to describe the singular involvement that occurs in psychiatry between a psychoanalyst and a patient," he points out that "it is readily applicable to biography." Indeed it is, and its dangers must be recognized and guarded against, for, as Edel warns, your participation in the feelings of your hero should "be sympathetic rather than empathic." If your identification with the subject is a positive one, you may find yourself idealizing him or her—"wiping out the wrinkles," as Edel puts it. If it's negative, you may find yourself overemphasizing the subject's faults and failures and neglecting his virtues and successes.

As the biographer comes to understand his hero, he inevitably and often less than consciously merges with him. When the writer senses that this is happening, he owes it to his subject to perform one of the hardest and most necessary of the biographer's chores. He must force himself to pull back, to put his subject at arm's length, to achieve that detachment-cum-compassion which is the *sine qua non* of good biographical writing.

As the conductor of a writing seminar, I received this query from a student: "What about the old saying that 'history is fiction agreed upon'?" I answered the questioner by questioning him. "Was the Declaration of Independence adopted on July 4, 1776?" I asked. "Was Thomas Jefferson the third President of the United States?" The student replied yes to both questions and retired from the fray.

Afterward I was ashamed of myself. Obviously, I had won the battle by choosing the ground on which it was to be fought. Pure facts, such as "Thomas Jefferson was the third President of the United States," are few and far between. To the inquiring student I should have said that the word "fiction" overstated the case, but that, yes, much of history—and much of biography—consists not of facts but of probabilities: of inferences drawn from whatever facts can be found.

As the material for your book accumulates, question it relentlessly. This written word—this spoken word—this artifact: is it authentic and is it reliable? That it exhibits one of these qualities does not guarantee that it has the other. A letter plainly in the handwriting of its signer may be a tissue of lies or a monument to the shakiness of human memory. Contrariwise, a forged document may offer incontestable assertions.

The basic questions—Is it authentic? Can it be trusted?—beget further questions:

Who wrote or made the item? Crucial to your evaluation of the evidence is whatever knowledge you have or can acquire concerning the reliability, expertise, and biases of its author or maker.

What does the statement or the object say or imply? Close scanning of the hero's own writings helps you to comprehend how he thought and expressed himself. When a letter is rife with uncharacteristic remarks or manner of wording, the possibility of forgery can be considered. If a Roman coin is inscribed "500 B.C.," you are in the vicinity of a joke older than the coin. Nothing is more beneficial to the researcher than the presence in his makeup of a pinch of paranoia.

At what time and at what place was the author when he wrote or said it, or the fabricator when he made it? Whether the describer of an event was or was not a participant in it, was or was not a witness to it, was or was not in a position to witness it—these factors weigh heavily in your decision as to how to use the material. If those in the know are uncertain about the wedding dress supposed to have been worn by your heroine, it may behoove you to make sure that the materials in it were available in the heroine's day. The authors of *The Modern Researcher* suspect that considerations of this sort were "in the mind of the student who wrote in a comparison of Herodotus and Thucydides that Thucydides had 'the advantage of being alive at the time he was writing.' "

Is the answer within your ken? If handling the question requires expertise you don't have, solicit the services of someone who does.

How does this description of or statement about an incident or person compare with other descriptions or comments on the same incident or person? At times the researcher, like the detective, must cope with the testimony of multiple witnesses to the same development. Like the detective, the researcher scrutinizes all the statements, noting both the similarities among them and the contradictions. Time-consuming as this undertaking can be, it has been known to yield gratifying results. Sometimes, usually as a matter of serendipity, it permits you to offer a hitherto unthought-of interpretation of the development. When confronted with crazily differing stories and judgments, I've found it helpful to show my notes on them to an intelligent friend, asking the person to give me his or her offhand reactions.

What data should one seek to illuminate the significance of the hero's actions? Often the best way to bring out the meaning of an event is to place it in its historical context. In his biography of Samuel Johnson, Walter Jackson Bate provides a strikingly effective use of this device. Between 1746 and 1755— a nine-year period—Johnson and six part-time assistants produced a dictionary of the English language, consisting of the definitions of more than 40,000 words along with 14,000 illustrative quotations from every field of learning. By way of underscoring the size and grandeur of this accomplishment, biographer Bate noted that the ten-volume *New English Dictionary* that later superseded Johnson's drew on the assistance of over 2,000 scholars and required seventy-five years to complete. For my *Andrew Johnson: President on Trial* I had to describe and evaluate the impact on the public mind of a convention convened in Philadelphia shortly after the Civil War in an effort to create a new political party. Casting about for corroborative details, I consulted newspaper reports on the American securities markets. These showed that during the convention in the summer of 1866 such markets rose and that after it they fell. That finding, along with others, prompted me to conclude that favorable reaction to the movement was short-lived.

When are facts not facts? Often enough to keep on the alert for them. I'd like to think that I am not the only writing teacher to have regaled students with an often-repeated story about Sinclair Lewis. Having agreed to conduct a course in writing, the story goes, Lewis made short shrift of it. "Do you all wish to be writers?" he asked the class at the first session, and when every hand in the room went up, "Then go home and write," he said and walked out. How saddening to learn from Mark Schorer's 867-page biography of Lewis that not only did he conduct more than one writing course, but that he did so with enthusiasm, usually neither requesting nor receiving compensation.

Some readers of Catherine Drinker Bowen's study of Justice Oliver Wendell Holmes wrote to protest her failure to mention a couple of oldies. One of these anecdotes has it that one day while ninety-year-old Holmes and a fellow nonagenarian were conversing on the street, a pretty girl went by. "Ah, to be seventy again!" Holmes is quoted as saying. Bowen skipped that one on discovering that it has been told of several gentlemen of a certain age going back to the ancient Romans.

A less heroic biographer might have included the tale with a disclaimer. Not that the disclaimer would have worked. Unlike old soldiers, old stories don't even fade away. Who in the world is ever going to believe that, according to the only extant account by an eyewitness, Patrick Henry did *not* say, "If this be treason, make the most of it"? That it was said instead by his first biographer is an example of how the teller of lives can contribute to the infrastructure of history known as legend.

One final suggestion for the biographer-as-sleuth: get as much of your information as you can from the horse's mouth.

Years ago, while gathering material for an article about a passenger ship called the *United States,* an acquaintance of mine was told by the builders of the vessel that it was equipped with "absolutely fireproof paint." My friend recorded this assertion in his notebook. At the same time he obtained and jotted down the name of the maker of the paint. Next day he called the manufacturer and asked to speak to the head chemist.

"I've been given to understand," he said, "that the paint you made for the *United States* is absolutely fireproof."

The chemist broke into a laugh. "Mr. H.," he said, "there is no paint ever made that will not ignite when exposed to a certain temperature."

CHAPTER 5

Form: Writing in Clusters and Other Procedures

IT "is perhaps as difficult to write a good life," Lytton Strachey concluded nearly a century ago, "as to live one." Strachey's awareness of the problems of his craft did not deter him from writing a number of lives that some of us still read with pleasure if only because he was a master of one of the more demanding skills that the biographer must cultivate. He knew how to shape his material, how to give it form.

"Structure, structure—more and more I see that that is the secret," Gamaliel Bradford wrote in his journal at the zenith of a career that included the production of a series of 7,000-word sketches—"portraits," he called them—in which, having cast off the "narrative scaffolding," he tried to illuminate the personality of his subject by reducing it to its essence.

But having decided that good structure was the biographer's prime concern, Bradford was at once seized with the thought that maybe good style was even more prime. Supportive of this likelihood was his recollection of a French critic's comments on *Madame Bovary* and the other novels of Gustave Flaubert. The critic thought Flaubert's sentences admirable, his paragraphs mediocre, and his books badly formed. Yet, Bradford mused, "many a scribe, who has a perfect sense of structure [form] . . . , has perished and will perish before Flaubert is forgotten." Which then was the more vital to the biographer: form, the shaping of the work as a whole; or style, the shaping of the sentences and paragraphs? By the end of his day's journal entry Bradford had thrown up his hands, admitting that he didn't know.

In fact, both are important; one could speak of them in the spirit of Abraham Lincoln, who, when asked which of the stovepipe hats given him by rival manufacturers was the better, disingenuously replied that "they mutually surpassed one another." Bradford himself noted that form and style "hang upon each other." The fact remains that, however deft your use of the language, many of the revelations and judgments you put into your book will never reach the reader unless you array them in an orderly fashion.

"The cradle-to-grave approach in a biography," a critic writes in the *Washington Post* "Book World" of 2 September 1984, "is strictly a literary convention. Only in biographies and never in life do we get to know about another human being in that consecutive fashion." What the author of these words is overlooking, I believe, is that if we could always understand the confusions of life, we would have no need for biographies. One of the purposes of a biography is to impose on those confusions some form—and consequently some meaning; and to this end the literary conventions are indispensable.

What is to be kept in mind is that while gathering our material we are working on the level of life, but to shape that material into a story we must work on the level of art. Life is one world, art another, and the writer who confuses them is going to confuse his readers too.

William Butler Yeats appears to have been underscoring this fact when he wrote that "Neither Christ nor Buddha nor Socrates wrote a book, for to do that is to exchange life for a logical process." When someone complained to Matisse that the figure in one of his paintings did not look like a woman, the artist replied, "Madame, that is not a woman; that is a picture."

Katherine Anne Porter, speaking of fiction, could have been speaking of biography when she said that a human life "may be almost pure chaos" and that "the work of the artist, the only thing he's good for, is to take these handfuls of confusion and disparate things, things that seem to be irreconcilable, and put them together in a frame to give them some kind of shape and meaning."

Meaning follows form.

Good structure is the outgrowth of a struggle between the writer and his material. The facts you gather take on a life of their own. They make faces at you. They thumb their noses. Most of them come drenched in overtones that must be sifted to determine first what they mean and then what to do with them. You push them this way and they squirm elsewhere. I recall my historian friend Constance McL. Green saying of one of her bouts with recalcitrant data that finding the right place for the stuff was a hassle, and that when she did find the spot, putting it there was "like pinning jelly to a wall."

The time to start shaping a life is not when you start writing but when you start researching. Perhaps you begin your study by reading a diary that the hero kept during the closing years of his life. You discover that in his sixtieth year he jotted down some memories of his childhood. Great! Information about a subject's early days is hard to come by. You write a lengthy note, taking care to print the names of persons and places.

Now comes the big question. Where should this note be filed? In a fact folder labeled "Diary," where no doubt you will put most of the information from this source? Or should it go into a folder slugged "Childhood"? With the making of this decision you have begun forming your book, for much of that process consists of bringing together in your manuscript those things that go together in nature.

When you start the actual writing you discover, as all

nonfiction writers do, that willy-nilly you must work in clusters of facts and ideas. Striving to organize the material, you try to put every fact and idea into a cluster consisting of other facts and ideas with which the one you're inserting fits better than it does with any other group.

These clusters are the fundamental building blocks of your book, and it is largely by tinkering with them that you arrive at a suitably shaped whole.

If some passage of the manuscript strikes you as murky and hard to follow, it is a sign that you have overloaded the clusters on which it rests. The remedy is to remove snippets of the material—gingerly and selectively—until whatever remains appears to have the requisite clarity and internal consistency.

As for the morsels you have excised: these can be discarded or tucked into other clusters in need of strengthening. Patently thin clusters, those that seem incomplete, call for additional facts if you have them, or for additional research in the hope of finding them.

A well-formed book does three things for the reader and does them continuously.

1. It tells him what is of primary importance, of secondary importance, and so on down the line. In short, it provides the reader with *appropriate emphases.*

2. It so links the parts of the book that each section appears to flow from the preceding section. Call this objective *cohesion.*

3. It gives the reader at all points a reasonably clear comprehension of where the writer is taking him. Call this *anticipation.*

Helpful in achieving these ends—appropriate emphases, cohesion, and anticipation—are a variety of procedures having to do with modes of development, with what the English historian Lord Macaulay called the "art of transition," and with the art of foreshadowing.

MODES OF DEVELOPMENT

You can tell your story in one of three ways.

1. You can present the events in the order in which they occurred. When you follow this, the chronological mode, you let time dictate the arrangement.

2. Or you can select what you consider the most significant facts and offer these in accordance with some preconceived plan. When you follow this, the topical mode, you let subject dictate the arrangement.

3. Or you can combine the topical and chronological methods, now merging them, now shifting from one to the other. When you use this, the mixed mode, you let the needs of the reader define the arrangement.

Am I suggesting that the mixed mode is best? Emphatically. Save for very short sketches, it is the only mode that will work.

It might seem that for an essayistic biography the topical mode would do. But when you examine some notable works of this sort—Sainte-Beuve's word-portrait of Molière, for example—you quickly see that what gives the impression of being a wholly topical piece is in actuality, and of necessity, in the mixed mode. Sainte-Beuve exemplifies aspects of Molière's mind and heart by relating episodes from his career, and though the other parts of the portrait are topical in structure, most of these accounts are chronological.

It might seem, too, that for a narrative biography, and especially for a birth-to-death book, the chronological mode would suffice. But to persist in writing an entire biography in this manner alone is to come a cropper.

No human life is so tidy, so uncomplicated, that you can reconstruct it by simply reciting the events of it in sequence. Some of the events were more influential than others, in the molding of the life, and you want to make that clear. Sometimes, to give a crucial episode the emphasis it merits, your best bet is to ignore the time stream temporarily and plunge directly into the episode, using brief references and flashbacks to acquaint the reader with the lesser events that preceded and engendered the one you are describing.

You need the flexibility of the mixed mode to satisfy two desires found in the mind of practically every reader—two strong but contradictory desires that your own experience as a reader will confirm.

The reader relishes the feeling that the story is moving steadily forward in the direction of ever more exciting events or more penetrating insights. This preference is as natural as those feelings you have about commuting to your work by public transportation—say, on a bus. As long as the morning bus moves toward your place of business, fine. But how do you react when without warning or explanation it turns and strikes out on a tangent? You get off—and if you jerk your reader about in this fashion, he too may "get off."

Side by side with the reader's craving for forward movement is his need to be told only one thing at a time. Frequently in any biography you have to meet this desire by shifting from the chronological mode in which you have been pushing the story onward to the more static quality of the topical mode. The extent to which you keep the reader with you at these critical points depends on how you treat the shift.

To return to our bus-to-the-office analogy, most likely you will remain on the bus if before the driver veers off on a tangent he makes an announcement. "Ladies and gentlemen," he says, "because of an obstruction ahead, this morning I'm going to have to take you where you want to go by a different route. Hold on, please, and we'll soon be back on the old familiar track."

By hypothesizing a biography, we can sort out some of the ways by which these inescapable shifts can best be maneuvered. We'll pretend that our hero is an American born in one of the colonies seventeen years before the outbreak of the War of the Revolution. His membership in a well-to-do family enables him to attend one of the few colleges then on American soil. No sooner does he have his degree in hand than the war begins and he finds himself an officer in one of the continental regiments.

He fights in this battle and in that, and after the war he goes into politics. At the same time he embarks with a partner on a large commercial enterprise, and when years later he discovers that his partner has become negligent about their contractual commitments, he contrives to obtain sole control of the business. Meanwhile his election to the state legislature has launched him on a career that carries him to the United States Senate and eventually to serious consideration as his party's presidential nominee—a movement that collapses when his enemies accuse him of using his senatorial position to further his commercial interests. Beaten in court when he responds to these charges with a libel suit, he resigns his Senate seat and spends the rest of his life in private obscurity.

The material on hand permits you to relate in sequence the events of our hero's life from birth to his twenty-fourth year. You cover his childhood and education in Chapter 1, his experiences as a soldier in Chapter 2, and the beginnings of his political strivings in Chapter 3. But even as he takes his place in the state legislature a new element emerges. Suddenly our hero finds in himself a talent for speculation. It is this that impels him, with the cooperation of a partner, to acquire half a million acres out in the Ohio Country, thus beginning a venture in the development and selling of land to settlers that the hero will pursue for the rest of his life.

Now your story has forked. It has split into two strands —the protagonist's political career constituting one of them, his commercial activities the other.

Do you continue to tell your story sequentially, intertwining the political and commercial strands? To do so is to overlook the reader's wish to be told one thing at a time. Obviously, it would be better strategy to interrupt the forward movement of your tale at the end of Chapter 3 and to devote Chapter 4 to a depiction of your hero's business endeavors in the West of his day.

Bearing in mind your reader's other longing—for forward-moving action—you render this shift as painless as possible by emulating the courteous bus driver. Either at the end of Chapter 3 or at the opening of Chapter 4 you warn the reader that now you must make a detour, tell him why, and assure him that your intent is to return him as quickly as possible to the old familiar track.

To what extent in this Chapter 4 should you spin the commercial strand? Sufficiently far in terms of time and incident so that when you reach the climactic sections of the book —the libel suit and the hero's downfall—you won't have to clog the flow of those scenes with lengthy references to or explanations of the business interests the hero has been accused of using his political office to advance.

Chances are you will not choose to develop this chapter in the chronological mode of the preceding chapters. You may find it advantageous to be guided instead by subject, describing only such incidents as answer the questions that the emergence of this strand has provoked. By what means did the protagonist and his partner acquire those half-million acres in the Ohio Country? What problems did they encounter in their efforts to dispose of them to settlers? In what kind of atmosphere did they find themselves on their frequent trips west?

In what ways did their enterprise contribute to the growth of the economy and culture of a portion of what was then the American frontier?

Naturally, you will want to cut off the spinning of this strand at some memorable point, preferably in a way that will enable you to carry the reader back to the Ohio Country when that becomes necessary. Perhaps you will decide to "cut off" at that moment when our hero learns that his partner is mishandling their contractual commitments. Concluding Chapter 4 at this point will make it easy for you, in a subsequent chapter, to transfer the scene of the action from East to West by some simple assertion, such as: "Our hero was serving his second year in the Senate when rumors that his partner was not honoring their contractual arrangements arose and he hurried west to look into them."

When you reach the cut-off, you may find that you have carried your story as much as twenty years beyond where it was when the protagonist took his seat in the state legislature. To pick up the political strand of his life in Chapter 5 and move on with it, you will have to close Chapter 4 with a sentence or two designed to carry the reader—gently—back to the time-frame within which you were working at the close of Chapter 3. The necessity of considering ways of doing this sort of thing brings us to:

THE ART OF TRANSITION

"Transition" is the name given to any means by which you link the events or topics of the book. Two examples of such linkages have been mentioned in connection with our hypothetical biography: the warning of an upcoming detour at or just prior to the beginning of Chapter 4 and the sentences intended to guide the reader back to an earlier time frame at the conclusion of it. What English-composition instructors call "topic sentences" are transitions in that they say in effect, "Now that Subject A has been surveyed, we can go on to Subject B."

To grasp what goes into the making of these connectives, think of your major topics as mountain peaks, of the spaces between them as deep and rock-strewn declivities, and of the transitions by which you move your reader from peak to peak as bridges. At once the attributes of a good transition leap to mind. It should be as level and short as you can make it. The best bridge is one that your reader can traverse so rapidly that he's given no time to become aware of the chasm yawning below.

Transitions take numerous forms, and some of those more frequently used can be described as transitions (1) by natural linkage, (2) by word- or phrase-hook, (3) by question, and (4) by time- or place-shift.

1. *By natural linkage.* Every topic has subdivisions, and if you decide to travel from Topic A to Topic B by this method, you begin by examining all the subdivisions of both. As a rule, you will find that one of the subdivisions of A enjoys a natural affinity with one of the subdivisions of B. If so, you delay your discussion of that subdivision until you reach the end of topic A; at which point you can transfer smoothly to B by attaching the final subtopic of A to that subtopic of B with which the final subtopic of A has a natural affinity.

Once the nature of something I was writing required a description of the activities of a Catholic religious order and then of the methods it used to educate new members. What became my "Topic A: Activities" turned out to have many subdivisions because the order engaged in many tasks. Among other things, it published material aimed at encouraging ecumenism, the effort by different religious denominations to cooperate with one another.

I opened Topic A with a discussion of these ecumenical matters and then described the other labors of the order—

only to find, on completing the topic, that I had boxed myself in. Unable, after repeated attempts, to find a bridge to "Topic B: Education," I did what any writer does in this not uncommon dilemma. Again I studied my notes, eventually finding some quotes that I believed would solve the problem.

Then I rewrote the topic. This time, instead of opening with ecumenism, I made no mention of that theme until I reached the final paragraph of the discussion—from whence I rode easily into Topic B on a transition reading: "As for this work [ecumenism], all directors of the seminars of the order say—some of them plaintively—that today's students talk of nothing else." This bridge in place, I was free at last to roam the corridors of the order's educational institutions.

Obviously, the use of the transition by natural linkage sometimes calls for extensive rewriting and always for careful preparation.

2. *By word- or phrase-hook.* This transition also calls for preparation—and my picking up the word "preparation" from the sentence above shows how it is formed: how by deliberately inserting at the end of Topic A a certain word or phrase, you can turn on it into Topic B.

Examples appear wherever the reading eye falls. In his biography of Sinclair Lewis, Schorer devotes a chapter to the impact of Lewis's first successful novel, *Main Street,* on its readers. He concludes this chapter with the remark that what the book said to its readers was "that all Americans everywhere make their march down the middle of Main Street, and that this is indeed the poverty and the pain of our lives."

Choosing in his next chapter to explicate the effect of the popularity of *Main Street* on its author, Schorer echoed the closing phrases of the preceding chapter, opening its successor with these words: "Sinclair Lewis was beyond poverty and for the time being was feeling no pain. Yet reports vary on his response to his sudden success."

3. *By question.* the lazy man's transition. It's so easy that

one is tempted to use it often—a bad practice, since the reiteration of any technique calls attention to it, which is exactly what no transition should do.

Still, the use of the question to segue from Topic A to Topic B has at least the virtue of brevity, and when you simply cannot dream up a more subtle contrivance, you write things like this: "And Congress—head of the rebellion even as the fighting men were its heart—what was Congress doing during these feverish opening months of 1776? The Congress was buzzing, bristling with plans."

There are circumstances under which the transition by question becomes respectable. As, for example, when your hero suddenly does something contrary to his usual behavior. You have pictured him as suave and ambitious. Yet when the president of his company summons him to an interview for a big job, he deliberately neglects to put his best foot forward and doesn't get it. How more naturally can you preface your speculations on this odd conduct than by asking: "What mix of past experiences and present fears prompted our hero to muff this opportunity?"

4. *By time- and place-shift.* Transitions falling within this category are useful for moving the action backward or forward. As flashbacks and flash-forwards offend the reader's penchant for orderly progression, they should be used sparingly; but when unavoidable they can be rendered tolerable by deftly worded transitions. Leaping ahead, we try this sort of bridge: "Jane might have enjoyed the comforts of her new home more had she been able to foresee the circumstances that three years later drove her out of it"; flashing back, this: "It will help us understand John's handling of the difficulties facing him in his new job if first we review the events that brought him to it." Contrast can add piquancy to a place- or time-shift: "But if at the office all was serenity for John, at the bungalow he shared with Mona in the suburbs all was turmoil."

My experience has been that as long as one is dealing with a forward-moving episode or a self-contained subject, the writing moves at a good clip. Delays tend to occur—time out for thought—when it becomes necessary to swing from one event or topic to another. It was the belief of Lord Macaulay that in the writing of history and biography, "this art of transition is as important, or nearly so, as the art of narration." To Macaulay's litany of the pitfalls awaiting the writer as he toils to shape his material can be added:

THE ART OF FORESHADOWING

In nearly every biography you have to provide the reader with background material: explanation of terms peculiar to the protagonist's activities, of customs and attitudes peculiar to his era. The writer who understands form so arranges this information that it says to the reader in essence: "I realize this stuff is less than interesting in itself. I am, therefore, passing it on as succinctly as possible and only for the purpose of enabling you to enjoy the goodies I have in store for you."

Nothing better serves the reader's fondness for forward movement than the frequent presence in the narrative of hints of things to come, of little arrows pointing to events or themes to be developed later. In a twenty-page section of Schorer's life of Sinclair Lewis I count no less than nine of these arrows.

"The years that immediately follow," Schorer writes, "the remainder of 1908, 1909, 1910, and on, a miscellany of false starts, lost jobs, lost hopes, loose ends, erratic wandering, begin quietly enough with a return to Minnesota that had been decreed for his health." A few paragraphs later, having described Lewis's first encounter with a famous author, Schorer writes that there "was to be at least one interesting consequence" of this meeting "many years later."

At this phase of the story a passing mention of the predicted "consequence" is all that's needed. You can describe the consequence in detail when you reach the time period in which it occurred. The trick is to foreshadow without forestalling.

To add that when you forecast an event you must make good on your promise is to enunciate a sacred rule: never raise a question in the reader's mind without eventually either answering it or explaining why it can't be answered. To neglect to do this is to put the reader in the position of a person sitting in a lower room of a house when someone in the bedroom above drops *one* shoe.

Speaking of foreshadowing—of these hints of things to come whereby the writer endeavors to keep the reader reading—it would be hard to surpass these sentences from Vera Brittain's *Testament of Youth:*

> On Sunday morning, June 27th, 1915, I began my nursing at the Devonshire Hospital. The same date, exactly ten years afterwards, was to be, for me, equally memorable. Between the one day and the other lies the rest of this book.

CHAPTER 6

Form as Beginning, Middle, and End

IN the opening of his portrait of Molière, Sainte-Beuve contends that the seventeenth-century dramatist was one of the few authentic literary geniuses of all time. In the remainder of the sketch he enlarges on this theme, using analyses of Molière's comedies and incidents from his life. And in the conclusion, he writes that "Reputations, future geniuses, books, may multiply . . . but five or six great works have entered inalienably the depths of human thought. Every coming man who can read is one reader the more for Molière."

Discernible in the structure of Sainte-Beuve's piece is a respect for the injunctions underlying the pulpit spellbinder's three-part sermon: tell your congregation what you're going to tell them, then tell them, and then tell them you've told them.

Curious how the form in which you compose tells you how to give it shape and meaning. Irksome too when you think about it. How much easier it would be for the author if he could throw things in any old way—and how much harder for the reader. "Art is limitation," G. K. Chesterton wrote. "The essence of every picture is the frame. . . . If you draw a giraffe, you must draw him with a long neck. If in your bold, creative way you hold yourself free to draw a giraffe with a short neck, you will find that you are not free to draw a giraffe at all. You can free things from alien or accidental laws, but not from the laws of their own nature." Just as you must write your biography in clusters of facts and ideas, so you must assemble these clusters into a beginning, a middle, and an end.

Beginnings usually write hard—chapter openings so much so that some biographers have been known to lighten the labor by resorting to abnormally long chapters (twenty-five typed pages, some 6,200 words, is a good average, with anything longer tending to the indigestible)—and *the* opening can be a case of living dangerously.

As you sit there, hands poised above the keys, waiting for some other-worldly voice to tell you how to start the book, you experience a fear and trembling akin to the stage fright that even experienced actors suffer when the time comes to make their first entrance.

Responsible for this *agitatio* is the possibility that unless you write these initial paragraphs at the top of your bent, the reader may leave you. Catherine Drinker Bowen, revealing that it took her three months of "unremitting toil" to frame the opening of one of her books, suggests that the worries besetting the author at this point in the writing process may be the means by which his unconscious forces him to dig deeper into himself.

Dig you must, for not only must you put into the opening of the book all the things the reader needs to comprehend and enjoy the sections that follow, but you must also do this with dispatch. Your reader wants to get on with the story—and so do you. Only by crafting the opening properly can you put the tale on the track along which you wish it to move. A well-shaped beginning is an off-and-running beginning. An ill-shaped one can stop you cold.

In what sequence you exhibit the elements of the opening —whether you begin with a scene (an action) or with statements of fact or opinion or with a description of the stage whereon the hero acted or of the times wherein he lived—whether you pick up his life at birth or death or with the doings of an ancestor or an enemy: these are matters that your subject and its peculiar problems prescribe. But every opening should do at least four things. It should (1) announce or foreshadow the main theme of the work, (2) meet whatever objections potential readers may have to your subject, (3) orient the reader as to time and place, and (4) engage his mind and heart.

THEME

"What is this all about?" That, understandably, is the question in the mind of the reader as he plunges into the introduction or into the first chapter of your biography. He is not asking, "What is your subject?" That he knows from the title. He is asking, "What do you intend to say about this subject, what revelations are you bringing to it?" As this is the question uppermost in the reader's consciousness as he begins reading, it is only good literary manners to answer it as quickly as possible.

Different subjects mandate different ways of doing this.

What could more clearly establish the theme of a book than sentence one of William Manchester's life of General Douglas MacArthur: "He was a great thundering paradox of a man, noble and ignoble, inspiring and outrageous, arrogant and shy, the best of men and the worst of men, the most protean, most ridiculous, and most sublime"?

In the opening paragraph of *Francis Bacon: The Temper of a Man,* Catherine Drinker Bowen quotes her hero as attributing his fall into disgrace at an advanced age to having "misspent his talents" by seeking positions of power in the world instead of retiring to the study where a man of his philosophic bent belonged. Plain it is that for the theme of her book—its major statement—Bowen has accepted her subject's perception of himself as an individual estranged from his own nature.

Malcolm X, at the start of his *Autobiography,* uses a scene to foreshadow the thrust of the story: "When my mother was pregnant with me, she told me later, a party of hooded Ku Klux Klan riders galloped up to our home in Omaha, Nebraska, one night. . . . Brandishing their shotguns and rifles, they shouted for my father to come out. My mother went to the front door and opened it. Standing where they could see her pregnant condition, she told them that she was alone with her . . . children and that my father was away. . . . The Klansmen shouted . . . that we had better get out of town because 'the good Christian white people' were not going to stand for my father's 'spreading trouble' among the 'good' Negroes of Omaha with the 'back to Africa' preachings of Marcus Garvey." With this opening incident the author points straight to the cause—black nationalism—that Malcolm X would someday come to represent on a large scale.

"Castes mark their children deeply, and as a caste the English gentry resident in Ireland were pronounced." Thus in his opening sentence does Philip Guedalla adumbrate the argument of his biography of the Duke of Wellington: that it was the aristocratic rearing of a boy born into an English-gentry family "resident in Ireland" that endowed the future Duke with the strengths that made him the greatest soldier of his day and the conqueror of Napoleon.

Much ado about theme, you object. I think not, for without one what is there to hold the book together? Facts do not speak for themselves. You have to find a voice for them, and the key word in that admonition is "find." No biographer intent on doing justice to his subject imposes a theme on the facts. What he does do—and should— is let the facts impose a theme on him.

MEETING THE READER'S OBJECTIONS

One finds at the extremes of the gamut of possible subjects two types that demand special attention.

At one end is the subject about which many books have been written. "What!" the potential reader exclaims. "Another biography of George Washington! What in the world can this author say that hasn't been said before?"

You must cope with this question. At the earliest possible point let it be known that you are either advancing a new interpretation or have found new information.

Fawn M. Brodie, in the Foreword of her *Thomas Jefferson: An Intimate History,* states that much of that book rests on "records, long available to scholars with access to great libraries" and that what "is new here consists in good part in what in these library collections has been passed over, or ignored because it did not fit into the traditional notions . . . of Jefferson's character."

Felix Markham, in the Preface of his *Napoleon,* reveals that since the appearance of the most recent of the previous books on his subject, "important new material has come to light."

Also in need of delicate treatment is the story of the obscure individual. When your subject is of this ilk, your introductive paragraphs must make clear why he or she merits scrutiny.

Brooks Hindle accomplishes this at the commencement of his life of David Rittenhouse by summarizing the contributions of that early American scientist to the progress of astronomy.

Years ago I picked up a copy of Dorothy F. Grant's life

of John England, the first Roman Catholic bishop of Charleston, South Carolina. I had never heard of the man, and it was plain from the way Grant fashioned her beginning that she was aware that she was dealing with no household name. Instead of starting with the hero's birth or with some crisis of his life, she begins with his funeral. On a certain day in 1842, she tells us, black bunting wrapped the downtown buildings of Charleston, the tolling bells of churches swelled in the air above, and at noon thousands of people converged on the Roman Catholic cathedral to pay their last respects to a man whose coming to their shores twenty-two years before had filled most of them with anger and apprehension. Having read this preliminary scene, I read on—eager to learn what manner of man was this who, coming to Charleston so hated, had left it so admired.

ORIENTATION

Nothing so irks a reader as to be left up in the air as to the when and where of the tale. One admires the skill and swiftness with which Elizabeth Jenkins disposes of these matters in the first sentence of her *Elizabeth the Great:*

"When Henry VIII died in January 1547, the most remarkable beings left in the realm were three pale and close-lipped children. One was his daughter Elizabeth by his second wife Ann Boleyn. . . ."

No uncomfortable leaving of us in limbo here. When? "January 1547." Where? In "the realm," meaning, of course, England.

ENGAGING THE READER'S ATTENTION

To pique the interest of a reader is to move him to some emotional reaction. There are ways and ways of doing so:

By evoking a chuckle or at least a smile. Paul Nagel opens his study of several generations of Adamses with these words: "Those who enter into the private world of the Adams family must realize that no one was more fascinated by the story of John Adams and his descendants than they themselves." And in the introductory paragraph of his sketch of Adam Smith in *The Worldly Philosophers,* Robert L. Heilbroner tells us that "A visitor to England in the 1760's would quite probably have learned of a certain Dr. Smith of the University of Glasgow. ... Dr. Smith was ... a rather remarkable personality. He was, for example, notriously absent-minded: once he had fallen into a tanning pit walking along in earnest disquisition with a friend, and it was said that he had brewed himself a beverage of bread and butter and pronounced it the worst cup of tea he had ever tasted."

By eliciting sympathy, as Elizabeth Jenkins does where in the opening sentence of *Elizabeth the Great* she describes the "most remarkable beings" in England at the death of Henry VIII as "three pale and close-lipped children."

By nudging the reader to indignation, as the initial scene of Malcolm X's *Autobiography* is designed to do.

By surprising the reader with an unusual choice of words, as in the first paragraph of Strachey's *Elizabeth and Essex:* "The knights and ecclesiastics who had ruled for ages vanished away, and their place was taken by a new class of persons, neither chivalrous nor holy, into whose ... hands the reins, and the sweets, of government were gathered." A less word-sensitive author might have written "the perquisites" or the "privileges" of government. Strachey's selection of "sweets" is noteworthy.

By making the reader gasp, perhaps by the employment of antithesis of the sort Irene Nicholson displays in the commencement of her sketch of Simón Bolívar, the South American revolutionist: ". . . born in Caracas on July 24, 1783, . . . he [Bolivar] was exceptionally articulate considering that he was also a man of action; exceptionally one-pointed in aim for a person so given to the storms of passion and . . . sensual love; exceptionally clearsighted for one so fanatically dedicated. . . ."

Or by an appeal to that love of a good fight common to all of us. Barbara Tuchman offers an instance of this in the opening paragraph of the "Prologue" of her *Stilwell*: "In July 1944, at the height of the Second World War, the United States Government officially requested Generalissimo Chiang Kai-shek to place an American, specifically Lieutenant General Joseph W. Stilwell, in command of all China's armed forces. The proposal was unprecedented: no American had ever before directly commanded the national forces of an ally. It was the more extreme because General Stilwell . . . was known to be *persona non grata* to the Generalissimo, who had previously asked for his recall." The scent of conflict intrigues, and the business of the beginning of a book is to intrigue.

Concerning the beginning, two further points. You are under no obligation to drop into the opening of a biography what might be called the genealogical entry—a review of the subject's ancestors. As Marquis James remarks in his life of Andrew Jackson, "The spotlight must be ever on the central character." The hero's ancestors merit attention only to the extent that knowing something about them helps us to know something about the hero. Genealogical information should not be wedged into Chapter 1 like a set piece; if used at all, it should as a rule be brought in later, at those points in the story where the hero exhibits traits that can be better explained by reference to the traits of his forebears.

Nor are you obliged to open a narrative biography with the birth of the hero. Appealing beginnings can deal with later episodes in his life—incidents that elucidate seminal aspects of his character.

Ancestors are not automatically interesting. Nor for that matter is being born.

Even as the business of the beginning is to intrigue, the business of most of the rest of the book is to flesh out, to fulfill the promises of the opening, to develop the prime theme stated or foreshadowed there, and to intercalate whatever secondary themes seem to be required.

As this section of the book, the middle, is the longest, it raises the most problems for the writer. One such problem has already been examined: the desirability of gracefully wrought transitions to smooth necessary shifts from the chronological mode to the topical and back again.

Another common difficulty is the gap in the record, the absence of adequate data about an important incident or person. Your hero, a well-known nineteenth-century American politician, had in another politician, Mr. X, a well-known enemy. Though their activities often brought them together, they rarely spoke to one another. Still, it is a known fact that one day, long after this feud arose, they conferred in private for three hours. Neither left an account of what was said and no one else was present.

As this incident is a break in the pattern, the reader wants to know more about it—but, given the paucity of information, what can you do?

Several things. You can examine the newspapers of the day. Perhaps they reported the event and conjectured as to its meaning. You can venture conjectures of your own, provided you can find in the records of the two men facts to support your speculations, and provided you make clear that you are

speculating. You can consult a bibliography of doctoral dissertations, on the chance that some graduate student in political
science or history has explored the mystery. Perhaps associates
of your hero and Mr. X left memoirs, published or otherwise.
You can investigate other aspects of political history, in the
hope of finding a similar situation that historians have
managed to explain. The significance of this analogous situation cannot be offered as the whole story of the one with which
you are dealing, but its inclusion will help give an unusual
episode the emphasis it deserves.

Or the wife of the hero dies. Theirs was a loving union,
but nowhere in your sources is there a word or deed by the
hero indicative of his feelings. Do you write that because of
the nature of the marriage he must have been deeply affected
—a superflous statement, if ever there was one, being an
inference that the reader is capable of making for himself? Or
do you, instead, study the conduct of the hero during the next
few years, looking for those telltale changes in his behavior
that measure the impact on him of a tragic loss?

It is enlightening to note how Catherine Drinker Bowen
in her biography of Francis Bacon fills a gap in the record:

> Anthony Bacon died at forty-two. Strangely we have no re-
> cord, no word even, of Bacon's grief at his brother's death.
> We know the event only through a gentleman's correspon-
> dence, which with businesslike brevity gives out that Anthony
> had died "so far in debt I think his brother is little the better
> by him." We do not know where Anthony is buried. We
> know only that in the spring of 1601 Anthony Bacon took his
> departure, with his lameness, his loyalty and some quality that
> won men's love.

Your beginning ends once you have told your reader
what you're going to tell him. The middle ends, often hundreds of pages later, when you finish the telling. Now for the
ending.

Perhaps one should say "endings," since, just as a biography has a main beginning and as many subsequent beginnings as it has chapters, so at the close of the final chapter it has a main ending in addition to the endings of the preceding chapters.

Gamaliel Bradford reveals in his journal that when the time came to write, he began by drafting a plan of the book —giving "special thought to the endings of my chapters." Describing how he went about his biography of Henry Clay, he writes that his first decision was to devote the opening chapter to Clay's religion. Having determined to proceed thus, he found himself thinking of "the episode of the great glass bowl that was presented to [Clay] . . . and was used for his baptism at seventy, or thereabouts." To Bradford at this point came the suspicion that the vessel was "a punch bowl, though no [previous] biographer actually says so." Then and there he framed what was to become the last sentence of his chapter—the sentence toward which the entire chapter would move, a sentence reading: "To be baptized at seventy in a punch-bowl, could one ask for a more delicious epitome of Kentucky life a century ago?"

What can be said of the ending of each chapter—that no part of the chapter is more important—can be said also of the ending of the book. This is important to the reader because it is the segment most likely to linger in his memory; to the author because it is the destination, the denouement of his tale. Until you know where a story is going, you cannot describe the route it must take to get there.

The ending of the book is that part you should have clearly in mind before you write the opening of your final draft—and keep in mind until you write "The End."

The sureness with which Philip Guedalla describes the death of the Duke of Wellington suggests that the biographer had this moment at the back of his consciousness throughout the writing of the book:

He seemed quite well on Monday; and when his servant went to him on Thursday morning (it was September 14) he ordered his carriage for a drive to Dover. But a little later he felt unwell and, methodical as ever, said: "I feel very ill; send for the apothecary." It was his last order, for the Duke never spoke again. He had been born beside the sea, where the long tide crept slowly round the bay from Dalkey to the hill of Howth; and the sea whispered still beyond the window of his silent room, as the tide ebbed slowly and the Duke sat on, a huddled figure in a high-back chair.

Many of the difficulties arising during the writing process are not solely writing problems. Some are research problems, and the handling of the ending tends to come within that range.

If you're planning a birth-to-death narrative, begin your research by reading material dealing with the subject's last days and death. How a person dies reveals much about how he or she lived. What a wave of comprehension sweeps us as we read that John Quincy Adams's final words were, "This is the end of the earth. I am content," that in the closing seconds of life Gertrude Stein asked not what is the answer, but "What are the questions?" and that Eleonora Duse's words as she expired, a victim of pneumonia, were *"Agir! Agir!"* (Do something! Do something!)

If the subject left a collection of correspondence or a diary, read these items backward, starting with the letters or entries bearing the latest dates. As an individual ages, he waxes reminiscent. Much that we know of John Quincy Adams's boyhood comes from sections of his diary written while he was sitting in the White House as the sixth President of the United States.

As death nears, a person inclines more and more to intro-spection. Of late I have been consulting the papers of a man whose letters, for the most part, are formal and unrevealing. "A bottled-up man." So an intimate described him. But in a letter written to his son from the hospital where he died a few weeks later, he speaks for the first time of the inner values that directed the course of his life.

During the preparation of my biography of Aaron Burr, I was disappointed by the lack of information about the lineaments of Sally Burr, Aaron's sister, whom he greatly loved. I tried the memoirs left by the legal figures of her day and the books about such people, as Sally's husband was a law teacher and a jurist. Nothing doing. I tried the local histories, books dealing with the region where Sally spent most of her short life. Better luck. The first comment on her to emerge from these was that in her later days she became uncommonly fat. Next came a remark from a townsman that she was "a woman of commanding appearance," a not unexpected statement, coming as it did right after the discovery of her obesity.

Finally, a thought occurred. For four years, long after Sally died, her brother kept a journal. Volume II of one of the published versions of this document runs to 453 pages, and on 429 appeared these words from Aaron's pen:

> I am more and more struck with the resemblance of Madame la Capitaine [of the ship whereon Burr was traveling] to my sister. The same large mouth replete with goodness, sweetness, and firmness; the same large aquiline nose, contour of face, and the two dimples; and when disturbed, knits the brow and forehead in the same singular manner; the form of the eye the same; very long; the colour not quite so dark. There is only wanting the broad forehead of ma soeur to be perfect.

If you begin your search at the ending, you may find it easier to write the beginning.

On this business of form, one further suggestion: if you find organizing material hard, try outlining published biographies. Note how the author ordered the parts. Given the same material, would you have sequenced them differently? And one further thought: the American philosopher and educator John Dewey found it "significant that the word 'design' has a double meaning. It signifies purpose," he wrote, "and it signifies arrangement. The design of a house is the plan upon which it is constructed to serve the purposes of those who live in it."

CHAPTER 7

Form as Summary and Scene

FROM the 29 October 1984 issue of *Newsweek* this comment:

> At a time when critics talk of "deconstruction," historians plumb the uneventful and novelists delight in the fragmentary and episodic, biographies and autobiographies offer an edifying oasis: the dramatic spectacle of life lived whole. Reading about the accomplishment of poets and politicians, of radical dreams and religious causes, offers inspiration—and escape. Above all, biography, even in its most skeptical form, remains a preserve of old-fashioned story telling. Readers weary of post-Modernist culture understandably crave tales with a beginning and an end.

Making a story of a biography or an autobiography requires dexterous handling not only of beginnings and ends but also of what fiction writers call summary and scene.

To write in summary is to group experience. To write in scene is to reconstruct it.

Both modes contribute to the telling of a tale: summary by providing most of the background information, description and commentary along with the requisite accounts of subsidiary incidents that might become tedious were they accompanied by the minute detail characteristic of a scene. Scene contributes by dramatizing those incidents which merit such attention.

Using summary, you can carry your hero around the world in a paragraph or describe the highlights of his career for a five-year period in a few paragraphs or a few sentences, depending on the amount of ground to be covered. Using scene, you can convey that sense of rising action culminated by climax and resolution that are the attributes of a story. The biographer of a military man is likely to summarize much of his subject's campaigning, limiting the scenes to those critical moments in the fighting that bring out the salient qualities of the hero or alter the run of events.

Summary can be designated as remote action and scene as immediate action. The words "remote" and "immediate," as used here, are not to be thought of as judgmental; they are merely the technical terms by means of which the difference between the probable effects of summary and of scene can be described. Because summary is generalized, it tends to pull the action of the story away from the reader. Because scene is singular, it tends to push it closer to the reader, imparting to the story the immediacy of a stage play or a movie. Had Marshall McLuhan seen fit to discuss this matter, I'm sure he would have called summary "cold" and scene "hot."

A true scene displays certain easily recognizable characteristics.

It serves the story either by advancing the action or by enlarging our comprehension of the personalities involved. Were the scene to be excised, something of value would be lost, something the reader needs to know. At the conclusion of a true scene our perception of the overall situation is different from what it was at the beginning.

A scene has a specific time and a specific place, and it is the mark of a knowing practitioner that, mindful of the reader's desire to remain oriented, he injects these elements at the earliest possible point in the development of the episode.

Every scene need not be a confrontation, but it should exude a degree of tension. A true scene is a little story within the bigger story. As such, it has its own background information, its own rising action, crisis, climax, and resolution. A crisis, as we all know, is the meeting of two forces under such conditions that one of them has to give way. When that happens, the scene arrives at its climax, to be succeeded by whatever resolution seems necessary to dispose of still unanswered questions.

Vera Brittain's autobiographical *Testament of Youth* offers numerous examples of summary and scene, adroitly interwoven to create a strong story line.

"At the age of thirteen," Miss Brittain writes, " . . . I was sent away to school at the recently founded St. Monica's, at Kingswood in Surrey—a safe choice because the eldest and ablest of my mother's sisters was one of the two principals."

The author follows these words with a lengthy summary of her years at St. Monica's.

In this summary she warps backward and forward in time. Miss Brittain arrived at St. Monica's in 1909 and departed a few years later, but "My aunt," she writes, ran the school on her own "from 1914 to the end of 1930, and . . . raised [it] to a high position . . . among girls' private schools. It has recently passed out of this category into the hands of an exclusively masculine committee, and now [1933] ranks as a public school." Summary permits this defiance of chronology, whereas scene—being "immediate action," taking place as it were before our very eyes—as a rule does not.

Miss Brittain describes some of her fellow students and in some cases relates what happened to them after they left the school. She describes the physical surroundings and some of the routines and happenings of the classroom. She comments on the movement of attitudes and customs since her schoolgirl days. "There is still, I think," she writes, "not enough recognition by teachers of the fact that the desire to think—which is fundamentally a moral problem—must be induced before the power is developed. Most people, whether men or women, wish above all else to be comfortable; and thought is a preeminently uncomfortable process; it brings to the individual far more suffering than happiness in a semi-civilized world which still goes to war, still encourages the production of unwanted . . . children by exhausted mothers, and still compels married partners who hate one another to live together in the name of morality."

For fourteen pages this summary proceeds, to be capped by a two-page scene as follows:

> At the end of one school term, I had been as usual shepherded by a mistress into the train at St. Pancras for the long journey to Buxton. Carefully observing the rule, which originated in contemporary White Slave Traffic alarms, that we were never to travel in carriages alone with men, she selected a compartment in which the one male passenger was safely accompanied by a respectable elderly female. Unfortunately at Kettering, the first stop after we left St. Pancras, the elderly female got out, and immediately the train started again the strange man, a swarthy, black-haired individual of the commercial-traveller class, with rolling eyes and large hairy hands, came over from his corner and sat down beside me.
>
> "I was waiting for that old cat to get out so that we could have a nice little talk," he promisingly began.
>
> More alarmed than I allowed myself to appear, I looked helplessly at the closed door leading to the corridor, but though its very existence protected me better than I realised, it was completely cut off by my companion's insinuating bulk.
>
> "I see you're going to Buxton," he continued, looking at my initialled suitcase. "How I wish I hadn't got to get out at Leicester! Now won't you just tell me your name?"

Encouraged by the mention of Leicester, which was only another half-hour's journey, I responded inventively that my name was Violet Brown and that I didn't live in Buxton but was only going there for a week to stay with friends—a fabrication inspired by the nightmarish fear that this apparition might suddenly appear in search of me on our own front doorstep.

"And how old are you?" he inquired, pressing closer, and looked disappointed when I answered truthfully that I was fourteen.

"Why," he exclaimed, "you're such a pretty little girl—I thought you must be quite seventeen! When you get home you must send me your photograph—" and he squeezed me still further into the corner.

It was then I realised that the train, upon which I was depending to convey me to Leicester and salvation, had suddenly come to a standstill. Some shouts were raised along the line; my enemy heard them, and informed me with satisfaction that we had broken down, and could not possibly get to Leicester for over an hour.

"Now what a lucky thing we're together!" he said softly, and took my hand—a grubby enough schoolgirl's fist, with ink-stained nails chipped by games and amateur gardening. "Pretty little girls like you shouldn't bite their nails," he murmured playfully, examining my fingers. "You'll stop biting them to please me, won't you—and give me a kiss to show that we're pals?"

The leering black eyes, the pawing hands and the alcoholic breath combined with the train's delay to drive me into a panic. Suddenly desperate, and probably more muscular than my tormentor had anticipated, I flung myself with an immense effort out of his encroaching arms, and dashed frantically into the corridor. The subdued middle-aged woman into whose compartment I blindly stumbled, flushed and hatless, regarded me with amazement, but she accepted my incoherent tale of an "awful man" and pacified my agitation by giving me a share of her luncheon sandwiches. When, after quite an hour's breakdown, we did at last pass Leicester, she went with me to retrieve my suitcase from the compartment in which I still feared to see my swarthy assailant, but he had gone.

I never related this incident to my family—the thought of the hullabaloo that would follow, of the fuss that would be made both at home and at school whenever I had to travel alone, filled me with too great a distaste—but so deep was the repugnance aroused in me that I remember it as clearly as though it had happened last week. It was not, however, until the summer of 1922, when from an open-air platform in Hyde Park I supported the Six Point Group in urging the passage of the Criminal Law Amendment Bill by the House of Commons, that I realised the existence, as legal conceptions, of indecent assault and the age of consent.

To cast one's eyes over the passage just quoted is to see that it exhibits the essentials of a true scene.

The time is stated at the very beginning: "At the end of one school term." So is the place: the compartment of a train traveling northward from London.

The informational background is laid in neatly: "Carefully observing the rule, which originated in contemporary White Slave Traffic alarms, that we were never to travel in carriages alone with men, she [the girl's schoolmistress] selected a compartment in which the one male passenger was safely accompanied by a respectable elderly female."

The rising action gets under way promptly. At the train's first stop, the elderly female departs and the male passenger begins making advances, precipitating a crisis for his fourteen-year-old victim: "The leering black eyes, the pawing hands and the alcoholic breath combined with the train's delay to drive me into a panic."

Then the climax: "Suddenly desperate, . . . I flung myself with an immense effort out of his encroaching arms, and dashed frantically into the corridor."

Follows the resolution: the discovery that the offending

male is no longer on the train, the girl's decision not to relate the incident to her family, and her belated realization of its significance.

A skillful intertwining of summary and scene can not only help the biographer construct a strong story, it can also help him to make clear to the reader what is of primary importance, of secondary importance, and so on down the line.

To summarize a development is to suggest that it is not of primary status. To devote a scene to it is to suggest that it is. Sometimes, in other words, the biographer can use a scene to help achieve the emphasis appropriate to his story.

Please note the "sometimes." A fiction writer invents his scenes and so can use them for whatever purposes he has in mind. Not so the biographer. He can write a scene only if he has the data for it. If he hasn't, he must indicate the importance of the event in some other way—usually by plausible conjecture, buttressed by documentable facts, and clearly identified for what it is.

One final point—an exhortation, really. Miss Brittain uses considerable conversation in the scene quoted above—a legitimate procedure on the part of an autobiographer passing on to us remembered action. A biographer, however, can use only such dialogue as he finds on the record. In biographical writing, made-up conversation, its appearance in a few otherwise excellent biographies notwithstanding, is a no-no. One should bring to his work all the imagination he can—but, as Leon Edel has said, it must be "imagination of form" only, never imagination of substance.

CHAPTER 8

Of Style and Tone

To the writer, what is style?

E. B. White calls it one of the "higher mysteries" in the closing chapter of his and William Strunk, Jr.'s *The Elements of Style,* a little book, 7 1 pages, that along with a dictionary and a thesaurus belongs on the desk of every writer. Who can say, asks White, why some combinations of words "explode in the mind"?

Buffon's familiar *"Le style est l'homme même"* is not so much a definition as a statement of the objective the practicing writer should keep in mind as day by day he strains to improve his handling of the language. Like Robert Louis Stevenson, novelist Henry Miller began his career by "playing the sedulous ape" to established authors—only to abandon this practice one day and write thereafter in his own manner. "The minute I heard my own voice," he tells us, "I was enchanted."

For the biographer, for any writer, the search for a style is the search for his "own voice," for a way with words that readers will recognize as his literary fingerprint.

Much has been written on this subject—much that we can read with profit. The authors of *The Elements of Style* point out that style is not a "garnish," it is not an adornment. Like form, it is a means to an end: the enlightenment of the reader. A good style materializes only as one practices writing, as little by little one learns how to use words as windows through which the intended thoughts and feelings can shine through. Barbara Tuchman in *Practicing History* extols the short, Anglo-Saxon word. The monosyllable, she believes, is "English at its purest." And Dwight Swain in *Techniques of the Selling Writer* urges generous use of words that can be confirmed by experience, those that appeal to our five senses: seeing, hearing, touching, tasting, smelling.

It is largely from these and other sources—from the common sense of style— that the following suggestions are drawn:

1. Any word or phrase that either must be used frequently or that you are prone to use frequently should be used infrequently.

It is appalling the number of sentences in which one must include that scratchy little sound "which." Any effort to eliminate it can be regarded as a service to mankind.

Instead of "The judge ended his letter to his father by discussing a business in which both were interested," why not "The judge ended his letter to his father by discussing a business of interest to them both"?

This sentence occurs in the introduction to a translation of a Russian memoir: "A good deal of the answer is suggested in . . . Pobedonostsev's growing hatred of the sweeping changes being introduced into Russia, which he called 'This whole bazaar of projects. . . . This noise of cheap and shallow ecstasies.' " Why not delete the unnecessary "being introduced" and the "which" by writing instead: "A good deal of the answer is suggested in . . . Pobedonostsev's growing hatred of the changes sweeping Russia. 'This whole bazaar of projects,' he called them. 'This noise of cheap and shallow ecstasies' "?

Dorothy Canfield Fisher has told us that her final act before going to market was to "de-which" her manuscript.

Other overworked expressions are "who was" and "who were" (when used for purposes of identification), "particular," "in order to," and "very."

Instead of "Albert, who was the king's brother, disagreed," why not "Albert, the king's brother, disagreed"? Instead of "Disagreement came from Albert and John, who were the king's brothers," why not "Disagreement came from Albert and John, the king's brothers"? Instead of "This particular expedition was not a scientific one," why not "This expedition was not a scientific one"? Instead of "Every apparently false clue must be checked in order to make certain it is false," why not "Every apparently false clue must be checked to make certain it is false"? Instead of "The money disappeared very rapidly," why not "The money disappeared rapidly"? Allow yourself two or three "very's" per book—no more.

2. Say what you mean.

Who of us in the throes of composition has not cast more than one sentence that on second reading proved to be gobbledygook at worst or a far cry from what we intended to say at best?

Among the recent submissions to a writing class was an article describing the duties of the "voting officer," a functionary assigned to United States embassies and consulates to assist Americans living or traveling abroad to vote in elections back home. Helpful to this officer is an organization active in many countries and known as Republicans Abroad. Thanks to an agreement between this group and the Department of State, voting officers are authorized to attend rallies of Republicans Abroad and to assist in the registration of voters. Having presented this information, the author of the article added this sentence:

> While this authorization applies only to those countries where only the Republican Party is represented, this is presently the case in 38 out of 45 countries.

Oh boy! So opaque were those words that I had to ask the author what he was trying to say. It turned out to be this:

Since, in their official capacity, voting officers must be non-partisan, this authorization is available to them only in countries where the Republicans alone maintain an organization—hardly a serious limitation, however, as this is the case in 38 of the 45 countries covered by the agreement.

Beginning writers learn quickly that saying what they mean is not easy, as witness these falls from grace in other student manuscripts:

"For the patients who were ill or troubled, Molly could change a whole bed without jolting or jarring." (One gathers that some of the patients in Molly's hospital were well, and that those who were neither ill nor troubled experienced considerable jolting at her hands.)

"She quickly replaced the blue dress she had intended to wear on a hanger." (Maybe this writer wanted us to chuckle.)

"Tanitabi, mounted upon a palomino, was a lofty and brave warrior," (One is left wondering what Tanitabi was like off his horse.)

"She had a highball in her hand, dressed in a leopardskin bikini." (No excessive nudity here.)

In *The Modern Researcher,* Barzun and Graff remind us that a good sentence conveys its meaning gracefully when it has these four characteristics:

a. *Right linkage.* Achieved by bringing together in the sentence those things that come together in the mind and go together in the world. From a recent student manuscript, this sentence: "Consular officers, like Rodney Dangerfield, are justified in feeling that they 'don't get no respect!' " Because of its faulty linkage, this sentence leaves the impression that the famous comic is a consular officer. What the student meant to write was that "Consular officers are justified in feeling, like Rodney Dangerfield, that they 'don't get no respect!' "

b. *Right emphasis.* The main points the statement is making should either occupy the opening and the closing parts of the sentence or, if that is unfeasible, they should be bunched at the close. Minor points should be dispensed with at the opening or buried in the middle. At its most effective, a sentence closes strong with no subsidiary clauses or phrases dangling like unwanted hairs at the end of it.

c. *Right rhythm.* Read the sentence aloud. If your voice stumbles or trails off or lingers in the air, rewrite it.

d. *Right tone.* Achieved by the selection of words and constructions true to the mood you are seeking to evoke. If you are describing a melancholy scene, combinations laden with "which's" do not belong in the sentence.

An anecdote puts Noah Webster in an amorously literary light. One morning his wife entered the pantry of their home to find Noah embracing the chambermaid. "Mr. Webster," she said, "I am surprised." "No, my pet," said the great wordsmith, "you are amazed. It is we who are surprised."

Say what you mean.

3. Write in live sentences.

A live sentence is one that does work. It flashes a picture or an idea. Whatever its length, however abstruse its contents, it yields its meaning readily.

Accompanying each of the sentences below is a rewrite that enlivens it.

DEAD: "The human condition today produces worry."
LIVE: "Today to live is to worry."

DEAD: "The anti-establishment attitude of today's youth accounts for the prevailing tension."
LIVE: "One reason for the prevailing tension is that today's young people feel hostile toward the establishment."

DEAD: "The common reaction is incredulous laughter."
LIVE: "Most people laugh with disbelief."

DEAD: "A biography of Oliver Wendell Holmes, Jr., should

indicate his place in the intellectual consciousness of his age."

LIVE: "A biography of Oliver Wendell Holmes, Jr., should tell us what the intellectuals of his day thought of him."

4. Trim the fat.

"Words, words, words," Hamlet said of Polonius's circumlocutions. All of us overwrite, unwittingly erecting a barrier of "words, words, words" between the reader and what we are trying to say to him. Hence the need for trimming the fat.

Accompanying each of the following sentences is a rewrite that slenderizes it.

FAT: "Each year about 2.3 million adults attain literacy through the help of existing programs."

LEAN: "Each year existing programs help about 2.3 million adults attain literacy."

The passive voice is fat. Many a sentence can be improved by shifting to the active voice. Wait! By way of practicing what I'm preaching, let me change that sentence to: "Shifting to the active voice can improve many a sentence." When, inveighing against the passive voice in a writing class, I argued that it put the reader to sleep, a student remarked, "Perhaps then it should be used in lullabies." Perhaps so.

FAT: "The center of town has become a depressed socio-economic area."

LEAN: "The center of town has become a slum."

When either of two words or phrases can serve your purpose equally well, choose the shorter and the more familiar. Mark Twain wrote of his mother, with understandable admiration, that "she never used large words but she had a natural gift for making small ones do effective work."

FAT: "Is your tooth experiencing any pain?"

LEAN: "Does your tooth hurt?"

As the Devil said to Faust, "No need to overheat your rhetoric." Pomposities are easier to write than to read.

FAT: "Numerals are used to identify the pictures."
LEAN: "Numerals identify the pictures."

Whenever you find yourself putting two or more verbs in a sentence, make sure you need them all. One or more may be fat.

Reading one's sentences aloud is a good habit. Often the ear catches flaws the eye has missed, and rolling the verbiage around the tongue will indicate whether you've created a live sentence or a mouthful of mush.

5. Lean on the strong words of the language.

On many of us, adjectives and adverbs exert a certain fascination. We write "sandy beach," forgetting that "beach" implies sandiness, thus rendering the adjective superflous. Or we write, " 'Hooray!' cried the boy happily," failing to notice that the content of his shout makes the adverb unnecessary.

As the authors of *The Elements of Style* point out, nouns and verbs are the strong words of English. Adjectives and adverbs are the modifiers and as a rule, therefore, of lesser potency. Use them when they're necessary. Fearlessly eradicate them when they aren't.

6. Be specific.

The more concrete the nomenclature, the more vivid the scene and the clearer the thought.

"An animal ran across the yard" is generalized. "A dog ran across the yard" shoves the sentence in the direction of concreteness. "A collie ran across the yard" puts it there.

Note the sparkle that concrete terminology imparts to the following passages.

This one is from David Donald's *Charles Sumner and the Coming of the Civil War:* "Weighing eleven and one-half ounces, the cane had a gold head; it tapered from a thickness of one inch at the large end to three-quarters of an inch at the small, and had a hollow core of about three-eighths of an inch."

This is from Lloyd Lewis's *Sherman: Fighting Prophet:* "So rich was the land that many a frontiersman . . . had quickly discarded his one-room log house for a double cabin, two buildings of logs connected by a roofed and floored space where the family might eat in the open air on pleasant days. Roofs were of oak staves, weighted down by rough timbers laid across them at right angles. Windows were of oiled paper; shutters were of thick lumber. Tables were split from logs, bedsteads were of poles interlaced with bark, bedclothes of bearskin and deerskin. Meat and vegetables dried on the rafters."

7. Be bold.

No sentence can say what you mean when you weaken it with what William Zinsser calls the "timidities," the waffling qualifiers such as "a bit," "quite," "sort of," and the like.

"Ned was a little large for a jockey" may be amusing, but there's nothing amusing about "Mary was *a bit* upset," or "After that, John did things *quite* differently," or "Genevieve was *sort of* puzzled."

Equally contributory to wooziness are irrelevancies and afterthoughts dragged into a sentence because they occur as you write. "When all the stars in the universe are considered, the difference in the range of their weights is small, though to be sure the largest of them is at least three thousand times heavier than the smallest." Pity the reader wrestling with that. What the writer meant, no doubt, was that "Though the largest of the stars in the universe are at least three thousand times heavier than the smallest, their number is so vast that the range of difference in their weights can be described as small."

8. Keep the language active.

Use sparingly the verbs that point not to action but to a

state of being. All forms of the verb "to be" fall into this group.

"The old man was fatigued" is an irreproachable sentence, but "The old man slumped with fatigue" evokes the sense of movement that characterizes good prose.

Of all the forms of "to be," "had" is the stickiest.

"Twilight had come," I write, "before John reached the farm. Heading hence from town that morning, he had encountered numerous obstacles. The recent rains had flooded the ford, forcing him to swim the river. At the fork in the road, he had met with a wall of fallen trees. Hacking through them had torn his already begrimed clothes."

I've read worse—and better. Having signaled a step into prior action with that first "had," I should have switched at once into the more easily comprehended past imperfect, as follows:

"Twilight had come before John reached the farm. Heading hence from town that morning, he encountered numerous obstacles. Swollen waters at the ford, the result of recent rains, forced him to swim the river; a wall of fallen trees at the fork in the road, to hack his way through. His clothing, when he reached the farm, was begrimed and torn."

9. Be original.

If a thing's worth writing, it's worth the effort required to find fresh language in which to write it. Stale language is as unappealing as stale food. To eschew clichés is to spare the reader words and phrases that have been used so often they have lost the power to excite or surprise us. This can be said not only of expressions of venerable vintage but also of those that are enjoying a harrowing popularity at the moment. Right now, for example, the eye glazes over at the mindless repetition of "innovate," "innovation," "insightful," "in depth," "meaningful relationship," and "life style."

Of all the sinners against good style, jargon is the most pernicious. To write in the lingo of your or someone else's profession is to leave the reader wondering what in the world you are talking about.

The major symptoms of a bad style are overwriting, dead sentences, adjectivitis, stale language, and jargon. But the major causes of it lie within the writer.

Inadequate knowledge is one. Only when you know what you're talking about are you free to speak with ease and assurance, with clarity and brevity.

Haste is another. Rewrite. Different practitioners do this in different ways. Some dash off the first draft, recording their major ideas as rapidly as possible. Then in later drafts they expand, rearrange, and polish. Others prefer to revise as they go, unwilling to proceed until the section at hand is the way they want it. Even work done thus can profit from at least one revision of the whole.

Dividedness of mind is still another—and the deadliest. Before writing, think the sentence through and confine it to the point you wish to make. Reservations too complicated to be embodied in it can be handled in subsequent sentences.

A good style is a heavenly thing, and probably heaven is where it's made. All most of us can do is our best, hoping as we revamp and refine that the lightning will strike.

But enough of style, a boundless subject. Of its companion, tone, what can be said? Where does style leave off and tone begin? That they "hang upon each other" we're all aware, yet they are different.

Style is so illimitable in its possibilities, so serendipitious in its effects, that it escapes definition. Tone can be defined. It is the author's attitude toward his subject, and adjectives can be assigned to it. The tone of a book can be passionate or light-hearted, earnest or tongue-in-cheek, preachy or relaxed, chatty or formal. One's style can in time become fixed, but from subject to subject tone necessarily varies. Clearly established in the opening paragraphs, the tone of a biography should remain relatively constant throughout. To be avoided are jolting swings—from chatty to formal, for example, or from earnest to tongue-in-cheek.

Different though style and tone are, they have one thing in common: their appropriateness to the material depends on the thoroughness of the author's research. As Bernard Shaw says in his *Advice to a Young Critic,* "Get your facts right first: that is the foundation of all style."

CHAPTER 9

Discovering the Hero

Of the many questions impinging on the biographer, the one requiring the most persistent attention is "Why?" Why did the hero say this? Why did he do that? From the taking of the first note to the writing of the last page, the preparation of a life portrait is an exercise in understanding, an attempt to answer the why's about the subject.

There exists, to be sure, a school of thought which argues that this is unnecessary, that unless the hero explains his actions the biographer should limit his report to what the hero said and did, leaving the reader to calculate the motives. But to present only the façade of an individual is to present only half an individual. The hero's inner self is the matrix of his words and deeds, and to neglect it is to leave the impression that those words and deeds happened in a vacuum. "Man is not what we think he is," André Malraux wrote. "Man is what he hides."

An essay by historian William B. Willcox, first printed in a University of Michigan publication in 1967 and then in *The Historian as Detective,* provides a graphic picture of a biographer grappling with a stubborn why.

Among Professor Willcox's books is a 1964 biography of Sir Henry Clinton, the longest-lasting of the commanders-in-chief of the British forces in America during the War of the Revolution—and the professor's 1967 essay deals with some of the work that went into that book. Perusing the Sir Henry Clinton papers at the University of Michigan, the professor discovered numerous instances of incredible behavior on the part of his subject. Sir Henry's "inveterate feuding" with his superiors and with the generals in his command, Willcox notes in the essay, "time after time defeated his own best interests." Still, it "was only one case in point. Another was his ambivalence about sticking to his post; for more than four years he tried unsuccessfully to resign; and then when he had permission . . . to quit, he clung to the command as if his life depended on it—and at the same time refused to exert the authority that it gave him. He was the rationalist *par excellence* in some areas, such as military planning; in others he behaved with an irrationality that I could not understand."

Willcox found especially bewildering a segment of Sir Henry's memoirs dealing with the disastrous defeat at Yorktown of his second-in-command, Lord Cornwallis. In the bulk of Sir Henry's memoirs, Willcox writes, "he adhered scrupulously to the facts, insofar as they can be established from other sources." But something was awry in his description of the Yorktown campaign. In this portion of his memoirs the general asserted that the government had ordered him not to interfere with Lord Cornwallis in any way, and "to prove this assertion Clinton cited the specific words of the command that he said he had received from the King's Minister in Whitehall. Here was what looked like established fact, and for years historians accepted it as such."

Willcox did not. He looked for the order that Sir Henry claimed to have received from the King's Minister. No sign of it in Sir Henry's papers. No sign of it "in the minister's copies of his outgoing dispatches."

What, Willcox mused, was to be made of this? Was Sir Henry guilty of a lie or was he the victim of that not uncommon proneness to self-deception with which all of us in this post-Freudian age are familiar? After further study, Willcox opted for self-deception. Sir Henry Clinton's "conscious self," he surmised, "seemed to have put out a smoke screen of rationalization, behind which he acted from motives so far below consciousness that he could not even discern them. . . ."

Alas, neither could Willcox. "The historical discipline as applied to biography . . . has inherent limitations," he writes in the essay. "Just when my inquiry was far enough advanced to be exciting, it was unexpectedly demanding analytic tools that I could not provide. To continue the quest I had to have help, and I . . . got it from Professor Frederick Wyatt, chief of the Psychological Clinic of the University of Michigan, a colleague with psychoanalytical training and a humanist's interest in history. We collaborated for a number of years on the puzzle of Clinton's behavior."

Once acquainted with the data, Professor Wyatt concluded that "in his quarrelling, his refusal to resign, his illusion that the government had been to blame for Yorktown" Sir Henry "manifested the typical behavior of the man who has never outgrown his childhood conflict with . . . his father. The unresolved conflict endures; the child as adult longs to exercise paternal authority himself, and at the same time dreads to exercise it because he is trespassing on his father's preserve."

Carefully set forth by Willcox in his *Portrait of a General: Sir Henry Clinton in the War of Independence,* this explanation of the bizarre conduct of his subject is enthralling—and convincing. So much so that I return to it in Chapter 13 of this book.

The present century has witnessed the emergence of a battery of new procedures that a life writer can employ to help him comprehend the external actions and internal life of his subject. Willcox was resorting to one of these when he sought the aid of a scholar versed in modern psychology. Other biographers of our day have found assistance in recent advances in medical and biological knowledge, giving us books bearing

titles such as *Napoleon's Glands and Other Ventures in Biohistory,
George III and the Mad Business,* and *To Be an Invalid: The Illness
of Charles Darwin.*

Considerable controversy surrounds these new methods
of personality appraisal, especially those deriving from the
theories of psychoanalysis. Some biographers favor the psychoanalytical approach and some do not. As this debate is both
fascinating in itself and pertinent to the intents of this book,
we will consider some of its pros and cons in Chapter 13. In
the remainder of this chapter the point to be made is this:
whether or not you avail yourself of today's new analytical
tools is for each of you to decide. If you do or don't, you must
begin that voyage of discovery which every good biography
is—that search for the unknown hero—by an examination of
certain long-established sources of information and by the use
of certain long-established procedures.

These sources and methods can be discussed under six
headings as follows:

PERSONAL DOCUMENTS

This category includes any items that the hero wrote or
dictated, or the writing of which was done under his supervi-
sion and reflects his views.

If he produced an autobiography or a book or two of
memoirs, you're in luck. Never mind that the autobiography
is self-serving and the memoirs saturated with venom for his
enemies. You can find correctives for these par-for-the-course
flaws in other sources. The point to be stressed is that with
these personal documents in your hands you are in the very
presence of your hero. If they enlighten you in no other way,
they tell you two things you want to know. How did the hero
see himself? How did he want the world to see him?

If he left a diary, you are in double luck. In an autobiography or a memoir he could rewrite his life, glossing over mistakes and claiming a foresight about coming events that he did not possess. But his diary, especially if it has been neither edited nor revised, shows you his reactions to people and events more exactly as they occurred. The more years of the subject's life the diary covers, the better. An extended personal record can help you portray the mental and emotional development of the hero as he traverses the seven ages of man.

With autobiographies, memoirs, and diaries, take care. Even in a diary, what you read is not necessarily what happened. Arthur Ponsonby, in the introduction to his *English Diaries,* describes one kept by a mass murderer who tried to cover his tracks by recording the horror and shock he felt on learning of the deaths of his victims. And from Gordon W. Allport's *The Use of Personal Documents in Psychological Science* (1942) comes this cogent caveat:

> The confessional diary, the type of greatest interest to the psychologist, specializes in "personality-making" situations, but like the autobiography, is prone to neglect the calm and happy periods of life so important for the stabilizing and socializing of personality. While spreading the emotions of distress or unusual elation upon his journal, the writer may not think to record the basic elements of security, trust, and happiness that knit his life to that of his family and community. That which does not pose a problem for him receives little mention. In health he does not write about his body, if happy with his family he takes the felicity for granted and seldom, if ever, refers to it. For this reason a confessional diary cannot be used as a complete revelation of personality without supplementary materials to help place its entries in true perspective.

If such a diary comes your way—an outpouring of introspections, of opinions and moods—make the most of it. No writing by the subject can mislead so long as you adhere to one of the ground rules of research: never believe anything you read or are told until you've checked it elsewhere.

As for letters, the more the merrier. They help you establish the doings and whereabouts of the hero, and as every letter is written to someone else, they also help you comprehend the nature of his relationships with other people.

Look for so-called "printed sources" of letters, especially those edited in accordance with today's high standards of scholarship. What a joy to find in such publications documented identification of practically every place and person mentioned. To every latter-day editor of a "papers project" every biographer should from time to time direct a grateful salute. In my own perusal of personal documents I've found it advantageous to provide myself with a checklist of the attitudes expressed by their authors. One such list, recently employed to guide my study of a diary, included a variety of entries, such as

Attitudes toward:
1. Self
2. Family
3. Friends
4. Fields of work outside the writer's immediate professional interest
5. Etc.

Years ago, while preparing a biography of Margaret Arnold, I used a collection of letters between Margaret and her father. Margaret Arnold, it will be recalled, was the former Peggy Shippen of Philadelphia, who became the second wife of Benedict Arnold shortly before his treason and who after the Revolutionary War left America with her husband and children to spend the rest of her life in London.

Most of the letters between Margaret and her father spanned the period of her exile in England. At the forefront of my mind as I began reading them was a question: how did Margaret really feel about her husband's treason and the way the British government rewarded him? In the hope of finding an answer, I included in my checklist these topics:

Attitudes toward:
***
  9. Politics
10. The Revolution

The checklist was instrumental, I believe, in my discovery of two lacunae in Peggy's end of the correspondence. Never in her letters did she write so much as a word about politics or the Revolution—omissions all the more remarkable because her father, in his letters, broached both subjects on occasion. The absence of any statements under the entries "Politics" and "The Revolution" suggested that Peggy's memories of her husband's treason and its aftermath were bitter—so bitter that she could not bring herself to discuss any topic associated with them.

PERSONAL ACTIONS

One method of ascertaining what the hero did—with whom, when, where, how, and why—is to draft for research purposes chronologies of the more complicated developments of his life.

The most useful chronology is one that shows not only what the hero did when, but also those actions by other persons that had a bearing on his life and that occurred during the same period or earlier. Such chronologies help you to sort out the elements of an intricate sequence of events; put the actions of the hero in historical perspective by bringing out the relationship between the hero's movements and other occurrences; and cope with the problem of cause and effect, since a precise listing of when things happened has been known to reveal that an event long regarded as having engendered a certain other event actually occurred not before but *after* the other event.

CONTEMPORARY COMMENT

What did the people of the hero's time say about him? The answers to that await the biographer in a capharnaum of sources: in the press of the day; in the letters, diaries, and other writings of friends, foes, intimates, and strangers.

More often than not, such appraisals turn out to be contradictory. One longtime associate of the hero is on record as calling him a person of infinite charm, another as likening his charm to that of a con man. You drop these quotes or paraphrases of them into appropriate fact folders, knowing that as you become better acquainted with your subject a consistent impression of him will take form—a picture of him in your mind against which you can measure the contemporary statements about him and in the light of which you can use them.

For a living subject or for one recently deceased, valuable data can be obtained by interviews. The secret of a good interview is diligent preparation. Determine what phases of the hero's life a prospective interviewee can talk about and frame inquiries accordingly.

It is plain that Catherine Drinker Bowen was thoroughly prepared when, during the research for her biography of Supreme Court Justice Oliver Wendell Holmes, she asked his colleague Justice Brandeis for his recollections of the years when both he and Holmes were practicing law in Boston. Bowen writes of this interview that Brandeis "showed no impatience when I asked for seemingly trivial details, understanding at once that the big questions are easily answered; they are in the published reports, the books. For the biographer it is the small details that are hard to find." At her request, Brandeis patiently described the offices where Holmes worked in Boston and some of the more interesting persons with whom he shared them.

SECONDARY COMMENT

To what extent should you use comments on your hero from the works of other biographers or historians?

It depends on what type of book you are doing.

If you are writing an essay-type biography, you may find it useful to quote what other students of the subject have said about it and either agree or disagree.

In a narrative biography, however, secondary comment has no place. Writing a book of this kind a few years ago, I argued with some statements that other biographers had made about the subject—only to realize after mine was published that I had committed a classic error. For one thing, the fusses with the other writers imparted a tone of stridency to the prose. For another, the intrusion of my own mind destroyed the immediacy of the action—that sense of *being there,* of closeness to the hero, of sharing his experiences as they happened, that a narrative biography should convey.

Well! We all make mistakes; and when your own get into print, all you can do is grin and bear it and repent not—and repeat not. As Barbara Tuchman has written, if you must "argue the evidence," do so in your reference notes.

LIKENESSES

On hearing someone say that no man is responsible for his physical appearance, Lincoln's Secretary of War, Edwin M. Stanton, observed that "the contrary" was true, that from about the age of fifty on a man is responsible for his face and that his whole character can be read in it.

So convinced of this was Emil Ludwig that for his lives of Goethe, Napoleon, and others he surrounded himself with pictures of them. Ludwig called likenesses "important original sources," writing that "I must know [the subject's] . . . portraits at all ages," and that from those of Rembrandt "I have derived more knowledge of the chiaroscuro of the human soul than from all the poets."

Bowen has suggested that before describing the old age of the hero or heroine, the young or middle-aged biographer examine good paintings of the elderly. She mentions with approval those of Rembrandt and Holbein, observing that some of the great artists were "ruthless in their portraiture of the old" and that "they're the ones to study."

My own experience has been that portraits and photos are of only limited value. Still, it is not a bad idea to procure a few likenesses of your hero, one from childhood, one from the beginning of adulthood, one from middle age, and one from old age. Affixed to the wall over your desk, they will remind you that as the years roll on a person changes.

For a list of publications containing pictures of historical individuals, consult the *Guide to Reference Books;* the National Portrait Gallery maintains a catalog showing where prints of famous Americans can be obtained; and the *National Cyclopedia of American Biography* uses a picture with practically every one of its thousands of entries.

CREATIVE WORKS

Under some conditions any form of creative work— drama or musical composition, statue or painting—can tell the life writer something he needs to know. Imaginative writings descriptive of the hero's time and place, especially those produced during the hero's lifetime, can be a source of corroborative details, of those touches of colorful fact that heighten an episode or help reveal a personality.

For some of her books Tuchman borrowed details of this sort from Marcel Proust's *Remembrance of Things Past,* Blasco-Ibáñez's *The Four Horsemen of the Apocalypse,* and H. G. Wells's *Mr. Britling Sees It Through.* "To determine what may justifiably be used from a novel," she writes in her *Practicing History,* "one applies the same criterion as for any nonfictional account: If a particular item fits with what one knows of the time, the place, the circumstances, and the people, it is acceptable; otherwise not." For one of her biographies Bowen found useful the reading of historical novels pertinent to the time and place of her subject.

For anyone undertaking what is called the literary biography—one dealing with a poet, a novelist, or a dramatist—the creative works of the subject become a primary source. They also raise problems. For to the literary biographer falls the exacting task of ascertaining what is truly autobiographical in the subject's imaginative writings, as distinct from what is invented or, as is more often the case, a transmutation and rearrangement of experience for literary purposes.

Illustrative of the care that the literary biographer must exercise in seeking his hero in the hero's fictional works is the use that some of the biographers of Herman Melville have made of *Redburn,* Melville's fourth novel.

Writing in the 1920's and 1930's, students of Melville, confronted by a dearth of information about his early years, rested their presentments of this period on the adventures of the seagoing hero of *Redburn.* A subsequent study by William Henry Gilman, published in 1951, indicates that this was a misreading of the evidence. Although, according to Gilman, *Redburn* does reflect aspects of Melville's youth, the story it tells was so romanticized by its author that accounts based on it afford little or no biographical sustenance.

CHAPTER *10*

Revealing the Hero

As the material that the biographer needs accumulates, he "discovers" both the hero and the other characters of his story, gradually building up in his mind pictures of them consistent with the facts.

We are told that when Sainte-Beuve reached this point in his labors he would shout to himself, "Eureka! I have found my subject."

It is indeed a moment to be celebrated, for it means that you have achieved one of the biographer's major goals.

But not the final goal by any means. In truth, all you have done is win a battle. The war remains to be fought, for now you must find ways of transferring the images in your mind to someone else's mind.

As for what the characters said and did—more often than not the presentation of these external matters entails only the sometimes irritating but always solvable problems involved in ordering the parts. But if you are to give us living, breathing people—as distinct from the handiwork of the taxidermist— you must take a long step farther. You must find ways of letting us know what those individuals thought and felt and dreamed; and it is this aspect of the writing, more than any other, that puts the biographer on his mettle.

Unlike the fiction writer, you cannot invent the inner lives of your characters; you can only deduce what they were from the known data. Nor are your own sensibilities, however strong, of much assistance in this process. Compassion, empathy, sympathy—these much admired qualities may help you to "know" your characters, but in themselves they will not enable you to share that knowledge with a reader.

Doing that calls for a proficiency in the handling of some purely technical procedures. You can expose the inner lives of your characters in these ways.

1. By extrapolating from a generalization as to how human beings ordinarily react in a given situation to how a character may have reacted in a similar one.

In his *Bloomsbury: A House of Lions,* Leon Edel uses this *inter alia* to suggest the unspoken reactions of eleven-year-old Leonard Woolf to the sudden and unexpected death of his father. As always, Edel is scrupulously forthcoming. He lets us know that although as an adult Leonard Woolf wrote many things, he never documented the feelings engendered by the loss of a beloved parent. To describe them for us, Edel extrapolates from this generalization:

> . . . there is no hurt among all the human hurts deeper and less understandable than the loss of a parent when one is not yet an adolescent

to the boy's mind, in these words:

> The mystery of death, the sense of separation and cruel abandonment, the deep-seated anger which one is forced to control —all this is accompanied in a small boy of Leonard's alertness by a feeling of discrimination and injustice. His playmates had their fathers. He had lost his. . . . Solomon Woolf had walked humbly with God . . . he had seemed proud and almost like a god himself. Was this the way the walk ended?

2. By extrapolation from a statement a character is known to have made about something at one point in his life

to what he seemingly thought about the same something at another point.

Again Edel, in his effort to show Leonard Woolf's thoughts at the time of his father's demise, supplies us with an instructive example. He writes:

> The family buried Solomon Woolf in a London cemetery. On the stone they engraved words from Micah which he had always quoted: "To do justly, and to love mercy, and to walk humbly with thy God." Leonard Woolf, aged eleven, found the words bewildering. God expected too much. He was not always merciful.

And then, in support of this guess as to the boy's thoughts, Edel tell us that "in his maturity" Leonard wrote: "I've always been sure that the heat of hell is preferable to the cold of heaven"—a statement that Edel interpreted, correctly I believe, as tantamount to Leonard's saying that God "was not always merciful."

3. By judicious use of the subjunctive, the tense or voice whereby we discuss likelihoods as distinct from actualities.

In his biography of William Tecumseh Sherman, Lloyd Lewis utilizes this device to give us a glimpse into the mind of one of his characters:

> A small boy like Thomas Ewing, playing beside his father in stump-lined fields of the Northwest Territory, would hear how as far back as 1785 the Government had sent troops into the new country to clear out squatters; how it had sent surveyors to plat the land and one army after another to quiet the Indians. He heard how the Government . . .

It's worth noting in the passage just quoted that in the first sentence the subjunctive "would" tells us that Lewis is speculating as to what went into the boy's mind, and that in the very next sentence he shifts to the more easily read past imperfect of "He heard."

Like "had," the word "would" is a troublemaker, to be used only when necessary. Indeed, the employment of the subjunctive to get at the inner life of a character has its pitfalls, and in the passage that follows, the author of a biography of a seventeenth-century adventurer falls into one of them:

> By pushing his way into the Guildhall one day, John could have listened to that man of tragic destiny, Sir Henry Vane. . . . This young firebrand . . . was now pursuing a reckless policy of constitutional revolution. His Guildhall speech, *if John really listened to it,* would *surely* have placed him in the boy's eyes as "the enemy," for how was it possible to accuse one's sovereign of wrongdoing?

That paragraph is overdone to the point of calling attention to the techniques being used. It could have been improved by removing the words I've italicized. As the first sentence tells us that John may or may not have heard the speech, there is no need for the phrase "if John really listened to it," and the "surely" further compounds the conditional.

4. By raising a question.

As in this excerpt from a work, the identity of which I have mislaid:

> As Smith read the cases in the social law library did he perhaps see that the practical effort to which his working day was dedicated was not unrelated to the speculative problems to which his evenings were given?

To be sure, the word "perhaps" should have been dropped from that sentence. Often, by taking care, you can suggest what a person is thinking without resorting to overworked conditionals, such as "perhaps," "probably," "presumably," "doubtlessly," "it can be taken for granted," "it is possible that," etc.

5. By shifting the viewpoint to yourself.

This procedure should be used carefully, lest the interjection of the author's voice impede the flow of the action. In her *Mary Tudor*, Hilda Prescott avails herself of this method to describe the young Mary's emotions when she signed the paper by her father, King Henry VIII, demanding that she deny the authority of the Pope and consent to Henry's divorce from her mother, Queen Catherine. Writes Prescott:

> . . . in a fit of amazed panic [Mary] had been false to her mother and to her mother's Church. She knew what she was doing when she made her surrender. I believe that she never forgot it and that in every crisis of her life afterwards she remembered it, and in the shadow of that memory, made her decisions.

It is astounding how swiftly and unobtrusively the author's "I believe" puts us in the mind of the heroine.

6. By reference to past or future actions.

In his seventy-fourth year Aaron Burr confessed to a woman friend that he was dead broke. He urged her not to worry, however, pointing out that he had thought of a way to overcome his difficulties.

What did he have in mind? I wondered, and almost at once something he had said eighteen years earlier combined with something he did three years later to supply a plausible answer.

Burr, I wrote in my biography of him, "did not specify the form he expected the relief [from his financial difficulties] to take, but a turning point in his life, occurring less than three years later, indicates the direction in which his mind was bending. Many years before he had toyed with the idea of making things easier for himself and his creditors by marriage to a woman of fortune. The possibility, it appears, had remained with him. . . . On the evening of 1 July 1833 he took as his second wife Eliza Bowen Jumel . . . , widow of a French-born wine trader and probably the wealthiest woman in the United States."

Important to one's effort to reveal his characters is the problem of perception—what fiction writers call point of view or telling method or narrative voice. There is no reason why the biographer shouldn't think of it in the same terms, since the handling of point of view is as crucial to his work as it is to that of the short-story writer and the novelist.

In a book published some years ago, I had to describe the scene in the British House of Lords on a winter day in 1782 when George III, speaking from the throne, conceded that the Americans had won their revolution and that Great Britain had lost an empire. It was a painful moment for His Britannic Majesty, and at first I was tempted to relate the episode from his point of view—only to change my mind as other possibilities presented themselves.

The London press reported the event, describing, among other things, the shouting crowds flanking the streets as His Majesty rode to and from the House of Lords. For a time I considered relating the event as the press saw it, but in the end a practical factor dictated a different mode of procedure.

It so happened that among the auditors of the speech in the chamber of the House of Lords was a merchant from Boston, Massachusetts, who later wrote down his impressions. As my book was directed to American readers and dealt with mostly American events, I decided to describe the King's speech as that one American witnessed and recorded it.

In the early morning hours of 20 June 1837 King William III died, and shortly after dawn an eighteen-year-old girl learned that she was now the ruler of England. At 11:30 that morning she presided over her first Council of State, and it is worthy of remark that in his *Queen Victoria* Strachey puts the moving scene not in the consciousness of the new Queen but in that of the assembled statesmen.

"The great assembly of lords and notables," he writes, ". . . saw the doors open and a very short, very slim girl in deep plain mourning come into the room alone and move toward her seat with extraordinary dignity and grace; they saw a countenance, not beautiful, but prepossessing—fair hair, blue prominent eyes, a small curved nose, an open mouth revealing the upper teeth, a tiny chin, a clear complexion, and, over all, the strangely mingled signs of innocence, of gravity, of youth, and of composure; they heard a high unwavering voice reading aloud with perfect clarity; and then, the ceremony over, they saw the small figure rise and, with the same consummate grace, the same amazing dignity, pass out from among them, as she had come in, alone."

What matters, Boris Pasternak has said, "is not the object described but . . . the light that falls on it, like that from a lamp in a distant room."

In what intensity of light, coming from what direction, should this material be presented? That query is ever present in the writer's mind as his manuscript takes form. Should you relate this incident as its participants saw and felt it? Or as outsiders saw and felt it? Or, as the scene develops, should you shift from one viewpoint to another?

With those questions you must tussle throughout the writing of the book. There are going to be as many answers as there are scenes to be written.

CHAPTER *11*

Autobiography

To base a book on your own experiences is to tread a path defined by luminous landmarks: by Caesar's *Commentaries on the Gallic Wars* (51 B.C.), St. Augustine's *Confessions* (390 A.D.), Jerome Cardan's *The Book of My Life* (1575), Jean Jacques Rousseau's *Confessions* (1781–88), John Henry Newman's *Apologia Pro Vita Sua* (1864), and—coming down to our own times—*The Autobiography of Osbert Sitwell* (1944–50) and *Growing Up* (1982), Russell Baker's remembrance of what life was like for an impecunious American boy coming of age in the Great Depression.

"We are all special cases," Albert Camus has said, and since every life is unique, it follows that every autobiography is unique. But this unarguable statement does not rule out the existence along the vast spectrum of autobiographical writing of certain readily recognizable types, each of them broad enough to embrace a diversity of manner and method and intent but distinct enough to be given a label.

Caesar's *Commentaries* is an outward-looking book, an account of deeds and those who did them, written in the third person and inspirited by the ruminations of a remarkable mind. Many a book has been done in this tradition, and we can speak of the category into which such works fall as the Historical Memoir.

Rousseau's *Confessions* is an inward-looking book, an introspection. The author reminds us constantly that such is the case. "I propose," he writes in the opening paragraph, "to set before my fellow-mortals a man in all the truth of nature, and this man shall be myself." At another point he asserts that his plan is to recount "all my actions, thoughts, and feelings"; and at another that the "object of my confessions is to communicate an exact knowledge of what I interiorly am . . . the history of my mind." This tradition, too, has spawned numerous autobiographies, many of them less introspective than Rousseau's but all of them introspective in intent and to a degree, and therefore assignable to a category to be called the Self-Study.

And Osbert Sitwell's five-volume autobiography, by blithely refusing to fit into either of the above categories, provides us with a third one, exhibiting as it does characteristics of both the Historical Memoir and the Self-Study. Let's call it the Comprehensive Portrayal.

Sooner or later the autobiographer must make a choice: which of the types is best suited to the material available? At the heart of this selection is the matter of focus. What elements do you wish to put at the center of your stage: yourself or other people? Your inner life or your outer life? Or is the material at hand sufficiently rich and varied to justify a Comprehensive Portrayal?

It is easy to think of autobiography and biography as kissing cousins, literarily speaking. In truth, they are not alike. Not, at any rate, to the writer. Granted the autobiographer finds himself utilizing many of the procedures discussed in the preceding sections of this book, but he also finds himself coping with a number of considerations peculiar to the form in which he is working—problems that can be examined under three broad headings: (1) Purpose, (2) Research, and (3) Principles.

PURPOSE

Like a biography, an autobiography requires preparation, a period of reflection, and it is a wise practitioner who during this interval puts purpose at the top of his agenda.

Purpose serves the autobiography in the same way that theme serves the biography. It provides the story with a unifying device. As has been said elsewhere in these pages, the writing of any book is a process during which the author must arrive at a variety of decisions. The autobiographer asks himself, among other things: What aspects of my life should I include? In what order should the episodes be presented? It is next to impossible to make these and other necessary decisions until you have formulated in your own mind exactly why you are relating the tale.

"For nearly a decade," Vera Brittain informs us in the Foreword of her *Testament of Youth,* "I have, with ever increasing urgency, wanted to write something which would show what the whole War and post-War period—roughly from the years leading up to 1914 until about 1925—has meant to the men and women of my generation, the generation of those boys and girls who grew up just before the War broke out. I wanted to give, too . . . an impression of the changes which that period brought about in the minds and lives of very different groups of individuals belonging to the large section of middle-class society from which my own family comes."

Other autobiographers, other purposes.

Russell Baker, in the first chapter of *Growing Up,* asserts that "children ought to know what it was that went into their making." Describing his own children as too young to be interested in much beyond the present, he surmises that there will come a day when they will "want to know . . . how it was to be young in the time before jet planes, super-highways, H-bombs, and the global village of television."

In the opening paragraphs of *The Autobiography of Benjamin Franklin,* Poor Richard regales us with no less than four justifications for offering the revelations that follow.

One is that it has given him "pleasure" to collect some "little anecdotes of my ancestors," and he now wishes to share these with his son. Another is that "Having emerged from the poverty and obscurity in which I was born and bred to a state of affluence and some degree of reputation in the world . . . , the conducing means I made use of . . . posterity may like to know, as they may find some of them suitable to their own situations, and therefore fit to be imitated." Still another is that by relating his life story he can "indulge in the inclination, so natural to old men, to be talking of themselves. . . . And, lastly (I may as well confess it, since my denial of it will be believed by nobody) perhaps I shall a good deal gratify my own vanity. . . . Most people dislike vanity in others, whatever share they have of it in themselves; but I give it fair quarter wherever I meet with it, being persuaded that it is often productive of good to the possessor, and to others . . . within his sphere of action; and therefore . . . it would not be found altogether absurd if a man were to thank God for his vanity among the other comforts of life."

And Chateaubriand beguilingly confesses that while serving as France's ambassador to Germany he worked on his *Memoirs from Beyond the Tomb* to keep boredom at bay. "Evenings in Berlin are long," he explains; "my secretaries leave me as soon as night falls. Sitting all by myself in front of a cheerless stove I hear nothing but the shout of the sentry at the Brandenburg Gate and the steps in the snow of the man who whistles the hours. How shall I spend my time? Reading? I have scarcely any books. What if I were to continue my memoirs?"

Must one always state his purpose explicitly? Of course

not. "Always" takes in more territory than any rule can cover.

Let the rule be flexible: know your purpose before you write and either tell us what it is in so many words early in the story or so construct these introductory passages that your reader cannot possibly *not* know what your intentions are.

Anna Robeson Burr's *Autobiography: A Critical and Comparative Study* yields an impressive statistic. Of the 265 autobiographers whose works Burr inspected, only thirty-eight neglected to enunciate their purposes.

One thing is certain: a statement of intent in the beginning paragraphs is the most effective way of meeting the question uppermost in the reader's mind as he opens the book— namely, "What's this all about?" In autobiographical writing, that translates into "Why are you telling me all this?"

RESEARCH

The autobiographer's principal primary source is his memory, and none of us needs to be told that the human memory is selective, distorting, and inadequate—in short, forgetful. As Freud has taught us, it tends to conceal as much as, if not more than, it reveals. "One reads one's past like a book out of which some pages have been torn and many mutilated," the Irish novelist George Moore has observed; and "I have changed nothing to my knowledge;" Yeats writes in the Preface of his autobiography, "and yet it must be that I have changed many things without my knowledge."

Much of the autobiographer's research consists of assembling props and jogs for his memory: birth certificates, death certificates, marriage licenses, educational records, military records, divorce records, financial statements, employment records. Today—numbered, credit-rated, fingerprinted, and computerized as we are—the amount of documented information obtainable is enormous. Indeed, in this country, putting one's hands on vital statistics is not difficult. A sensible first step is a letter to the Superintendent of Documents (U.S. Government Printing Office, Washington, D.C. 20402), requesting a copy of the pamphlet *Where to Write for Births, Deaths, Marriages, Divorces.*

Perhaps you need information about ancestors. You can advertise for such data in the classified pages of a newspaper. Ads of this sort appear with some frequency in the "Personals" columns. A recent request in the *Washington Post* reads: "Information needed on the Australian descendants of [name, address, and dates of person]. . . . Please correspond with [advertiser's name and address]." A list of bibliographies and other tools for tracing ancestors in the United States and elsewhere is available at your library in the Genealogy section of *Guide to Reference Books.*

Dates are like cats: now with us, now out for an extended stroll. But even the most elusive of them can be recovered. Say your memory retains a certain crisis of your life, an incident that you now realize greatly influenced the kind of person you've become. But just when did it happen? After Aunt Susie's death or before? Can you recall the happenings in the world around you at the time? What were the newspapers featuring? Or if you were too young to be reading them, what were your parents talking about? Was that the year when Branch Rickey of the old Brooklyn Dodgers broke the color barrier in professional baseball by hiring Jackie Robinson? Check the subject heading "Baseball" in the catalog at your library. Some statistics-crammed handbook of the sport will give you the year, and an examination of the *New York Times Index* for that year—under the subject heading "Robinson, Jackie"—may enable you to pin down the very day on which the crisis occurred. Or was that the year Neville Chamberlain went to Munich? Look up "Chamberlain, Neville" in an encyclopedia.

Most of us remember well enough the larger events of our lives, but what gives an autobiography depth and color is our ability to describe the feelings that those events induced in us when they happened—as distinct from the way our older self might react to similar events. We know that Vera Brittain is trying to convey faithfully the emotions of a much younger Vera Brittain when in her *Testament of Youth* she describes her first term as a student at Oxford in these words:

> There was a light on my path and a dizzy intoxication in the air; the old buildings in the August sunshine seemed crowned with a golden glory, and I tripped up and down the High Street between St. Hilda's and the Examination Schools on gay feet. . . .
>
> My fellow "thirsters" were the usual Summer Meeting collection of unoccupied spinsters, schoolmistresses on holiday, fatherly chapel-goers and earnest young men in sweaters and soft collars, but I thought them all extremely talented and enormously important. Had anyone told me that less than a decade afterwards I should myself be lecturing to similar gatherings, I should blankly have refused to believe him, for if I was in awe of the audiences, the lecturers seemed to me to be at least on a level with Angels and Archangels and all the company of heaven.

It is true, as Elizabeth Bowen has said, that we cannot wholly enter into the past, not even into our own past; but we can open our minds sufficiently to let at least some of the past enter us.

Diaries, if you kept one, and letters, if you saved them, can be enormously helpful. Vera Brittain uses her diary adroitly to recapture the attitudes of her younger days. Alfred Kazin attributes the "passion and beat" of his autobiographical works—*A Walker in the City, Starting Out in the Thirties,* and *New York Jew*—to his practice "since I was a boy" of recording his impressions of the life around him in notebooks. And in

Growing Up Russell Baker is able to give us a moving picture of his widowed mother's romance with an admirable gentleman because Baker still possesses the letters that the gentleman wrote.

Common sense dictates how the material assembled should be filed: some of it in folders bearing chronological slugs, such as "Childhood," "Public school," "Career," "Marriage," etc.; some of it under the names of the places where you have lived; some of it under labels reflecting the highlights of your life, such as "Accident," "Mother's death," and "European tour"; and some of it under the names of relatives, friends, playmates, husbands, wives, lovers, mistresses, teachers, enemies, and associates.

A suggestion, an earnest one: reduce whatever vital statistics you collect to brief notes. Put these in appropriate fact folders and store the original documents elsewhere.

PRINCIPLES

Anna Robeson Burr, in her classic study of the autobiography, calls attention to the Preface of *Journal of a Young Artist* by Marie Bashkirtseff, a talented Russian who died in her twenty-fourth year.

"The record of a woman's life," Bashkirtseff wrote, "written down . . . as if no one in the world were to read it, yet with the purpose of being read, is always interesting. . . . "

To write your life story "as if no one in the world were to read it" and yet to make it readable! Candor well expressed: what better precept can an autobiographer bring to the guidance of his pen?

Was the big prize you received gotten by cheating? If you're willing to tell us as much, you've passed the first test. Are you game for the labor required to construct a beginning, a middle, and an end, and to so blend summary and scene as to create a true story? If so, you've passed the second test.

A great autobiography, an English student of the genre has said, is a combination "of poetic subjectivity and ruthless objectivity." To say that such goals are difficult to attain is not to say that they are unattainable. Many great autobiographies have been written, and as long as people are interested in people, many others will be. One of my neighbors remarked recently that autobiography was her favorite reading. When I asked why: "Oh, you know," she said, "you make a friend."

CHAPTER *12*

Regional Biography

A one-man poll, conducted with the aid of the LCCC—the Library of Congress Computer Catalog—discloses some arresting statistics. Included in the holdings of the LC are 240 books on George Washington, 432 on Abraham Lincoln, 260 on John F. Kennedy, 131 on Martin Luther King, Jr., 19 on Geronimo, 16 on Mary Baker Eddy, and 34 on Marilyn Monroe.

Must we conclude from these facts that the cachet of biographical concern falls only on the famous? The answer is no. Every year sees the publication in the United States of books dealing with lesser-known figures, books that we can categorize as regional biographies—regional in that their subjects are individuals deserving of remembrance because of the impact of their lives on some geographical or institutional entity: on, for example, the state of Washington or the English Midlands or the city of St. Louis or a colony of artists in New Mexico or the University of Hawaii or an industrial corporation.

"Biography," Leon Edel has observed, "is a noble and adventurous art." Certainly the writing of regional biography is a worthy undertaking. Its authors preserve for us not only interesting minor figures (minor in the sense that little else has been written about them) but also little-noted segments of history—people and events, in other words, that might otherwise disappear into the dead-letter office of our collective past.

Like all biographies, regionals come in a gallimaufry of forms.

William H. Cumberland's *Wallace M. Short: Iowa Rebel* is a birth-to-death portrayal of a twentieth-century minister-turned-politician-turned-journalist who battled for the cause of organized labor when it was unpopular to do so, opposed the coming of Prohibition—going so far as to panegyrize the saloon as the "social club" of the workingman—and devoted his adult years to a furtherance of social, political, and economic justice. Although I grew up in the Hawkeye State, Short's name was new to me and I suspect I'm not the only Iowan, former or current, to welcome Cumberland's resurrection of a fascinating landsman.

Lewis Baker's *The Percys of Mississippi: Politics and Literature in the New South* (1983) and Robert E. Levinson's *The Jews in the California Gold Rush* (1978) are collective biographies. Baker's account of a family enlarges our comprehension of the changing mores in the American South, and Levinson's book enables us to view one of the great dramas of the West from an unusual angle.

William M. Maury's *Alexander "Boss" Shepherd and the Board of Public Works* (1978) and *Christopher Gadsden and the American Revolution* by E. Stanly Godbold, Jr., and Robert H. Woody (1982) are "and" biographies. In each of them the author uses his hero as a prism on a significant stretch of American history.

And Peter N. Carroll's *The Other Samuel Johnson: A Psychohistory of Early New England* (1978) is a psychobiography. Its central figure was the first president of what is now Columbia University, and its author describes the work as an attempt "to reconstruct an interaction between the man and his culture, . . . observe the formation of a mature personality, and explore

the subtle relationships between emotional, sometimes unconscious, feelings and more visible behavior."

Since regional biography is biography first and regional
second, this question arises: what needs to be said about the
writing of it that hasn't been said already of biographical writing in general? Several matters of this sort, I think, merit a few
words.

Regional biography vouchsafes a bright and inviting window of opportunity to the beginning writer. I would not want
that statement to be construed as putting the field off limits to
the seasoned artist. Many good regionals have been the work
of veteran authors, pleased, one can be sure, at the prospect
of breaking new ground and of rescuing from oblivion individuals eminently eligible for biographical attention.

The point is this: every writer, whatever his interest,
must serve an apprenticeship, and for the life writer no activ-
ity fulfills this purpose better than the preparation of a regional biography. The author who selects as his first subject
a person intimately connected with the author's own locale
launches his career, like Mark Twain's poker player, with
four aces up his sleeve. The feel and the spirit of the place
are already in his bones and need not be acquired at second
hand by research.

To get down to cases: Let's imagine a curious and lively-
minded auctorial novice—a young person perhaps, or perhaps
an older one recently retired from a job and eager to scratch a
longtime itch to write. Let's give our tyro a name—Robert will
do—and assume that Robert has elected to go the regional-
biography route.

We know, of course, what his immediate needs are: a
subject and a cache of rich subject matter. What then should
be Robert's first step? A visit, probably followed by other
visits, to one or more of the historical archives within comfortable traveling distance of his home—there to browse among
the manuscript holdings until he finds both an exciting subject

and enough primary material to put his research solidly under way.

Where historical archives are concerned, the writer working in the United States is twice—nay, fifty times blessed. In no other country are more people more diligently engaged in gathering and storing the data and the artifacts of their past. My own state alone, Virginia, maintains thirty institutions devoted to this work, and every other state has a goodly number.

Published in 1936, the first edition of what is now known as the *Directory: Historical Societies and Agencies in the United States and Canada* displayed 583 entries. Published in 1982, the current edition of this usefully organized reference book lists 5,865 such institutions! And many of the some 4,000 American archives are continuously adding to their collections. Some limit themselves to their own areas, others encompass the country, and still others the world.

As for the times covered—this ranges greatly. The Adam East Museum in Moses Lake, Washington, describes its "period of collection" as running from "prehistoric" to 1918. The splendidly run Historical Society of Pennsylvania in Philadelphia gives its period as "1492–present," and the White House Association of Montgomery, Alabama, confines its acquisitions to the year 1861.

What a luxuriant grazing ground for the biographer these organizations can be. For a book written years ago I needed a little information on Francis Hopkinson, a signer of the Declaration of Independence, musical composer, and literary light of the Revolutionary era. Finding-tools at the Library of Congress located his papers at the Historical Society of Pennsylvania, and I took myself thither.

No sooner had the material I ordered reached my desk in the society's reading room than one of the librarians was at my elbow, an eager expression on her face.

"Oh, Mr. Lomask," she said, "I do hope you're planning to do something serious about Mr. Hopkinson."

"Would that please you?" I asked.

"Oh, indeed," she replied. "We've had his papers ever so long and we're dying for someone to make some real use of them."

I understood her feelings. America's bulging historical societies—to say nothing of the many lesser archives tucked into gloomy corners of county courthouses and city halls—are underused. One can only hope that in the years ahead more and more books will be coming out of these storehouses of information.

While we're on the matter of regionals, I hope no writer or would-be writer of them will take amiss an earnest adjuration. Write, please, not as an antiquarian but as a biographer. Everyone, I am sure, appreciates the difference. The antiquarian collects and records material; the biographer endeavors to interpret and shape it. He writes to a reader, to an invisible somebody sitting on the far side of his desk. He brings to this effort a desire to tell a story; to create a beginning, a middle, and an end; to achieve a sensitive balance of summary and scene; and on every page he evinces a profound respect for the niceties of the language.

Some regional biographies are, shall we say, less regional than others. Fusspots about definitions probably classify Geoffrey Wolff's *Black Sun* as a literary biography—a recounting of the life of one Harry Crosby: Boston patrician, member of the American literary scene in Paris in the 1920's, awful poet, imaginative publisher, lover of beautiful women, and a suicide at thirty-one. Regional or literary, *Black Sun* can be cited as a shining example of a graceful, even elegant, reconstruction of the life of a minor figure.

CHAPTER *13*

Psychobiography

To look at the provocative world of psychobiography from the standpoint of the writer requires

a definition of the term,
and
a consideration of problems special to psychobiographical writing as brought out in the current debate over its merits.

DEFINITION

As readers of biography know, common-sense psychology—the understanding of human nature that comes with living—has been a staple of good biographies for as far back as such things go.

Plutarch, writing in the first century A.D., said of his accounts of forty-six ancient Greeks and Romans: "My design is not to write histories, but lives . . . the most glorious exploits do not always furnish us with the clearest discoveries of virtue or vice in men; sometimes a matter of less moment, an expression or a jest, informs us better of their characters and inclinations. . . ."

Sainte-Beuve, writing in the nineteenth century, exhibited throughout his *Portraits* a keen sense of the strange ways of the human psyche.

And Sigmund Freud was a teenager in 1871 when James Russell Lowell "analyzed" Thoreau in a sketch: "Those who most loudly advertise their passion for seclusion and their intimacy with nature—have been mostly sentimentalists, unreal men, misanthropes on the spindle side, solacing an uneasy suspicion of themselves by professing contempt for their kind. . . ."

What then distinguishes today's psychobiographies from yesterday's psychologically informed biographies? Where do we draw the line?

We draw it at Freud, at the emergence in the late nineteenth century of psychoanalysis, followed in the present century by other new ways of studying human behavior—theoretical systems subsumed under a variety of terms, such as behaviorism, phenomenology, and developmental psychology.

Definitions of psychobiography abound in the extensive literature on the subject. Of these, the most useful for our purposes is the one supplied by William McKinley Runyan in his *Life Histories and Psychobiography: Explorations in Theory and Method* (1982). What puts psychobiography in a class by itself, according to Runyan, is the conscious employment by its authors of the perceptions associated with one or more of today's "explicit or formal" systems of psychological thought and investigation.

To date, most psychobiographers have turned to the theories of psychoanalysis, making considerable use of the more widely accepted Freudian concepts—notably, the unconscious, the Oedipus complex, the observed capacity of the individual for rationalization and other defense mechanisms, the idea that all human behavior is "motivated, adaptive, and determined," and the view of the human psyche as consisting of ego, id, and superego.

"The existence of an unconscious with a symbolic language different from that of conscious everyday life . . . ," Frank E. Manuel writes in his *A Portrait of Isaac Newton,* "is a fundamental assumption of this study. Should the unconscious perchance not exist, one of the underpinnings of the book collapses."

That many writers have found their psychological "underpinnings" in the science of man fathered by Freud is understandable. Psychoanalysis focuses forcefully on motives and emotions. So does biography. The marriage of the two, although unsteady and troubled as many marriages are, would seem to have been made in heaven.

SPECIAL PROBLEMS

Is psychobiography as defined by Runyan the wave of the future or a passing fad?

That question has been the subject of ardent debate ever since the publication in 1910 of the first pure example of the genre, Freud's *Leonardo da Vinci and a Memory of His Childhood.*

In his *Life Histories and Psychobiography,* Runyan summarizes in detail the pros and cons of this controversy. In these pages we will limit ourselves to the four most frequently advanced criticisms, including under each heading one or more possible ways of solving or at any rate minimizing the difficulty to which the criticism points.

Faulty or Inadequate Evidence

A common complaint about psychobiography takes this form: a psychotherapist talks to his patient and has at his disposal techniques for getting at the patient's inner life—his feelings, dreams, and fantasies.

The biographer cannot function in this fashion. "The

patient is absent," writes Jacques Barzun, "and the clues he
may have left to his once living psyche are the product of
chance. Diaries, letters, literary work form a random record.
. . . 'Dream-material' is extremely rare. Compared to the
volumes of data elicited under therapy . . . this trickle from
written remains seems negligible."

Runyan finds this objection valid and urges us as writers
to take it seriously—to regard it not as an argument against
psychobiography, however, but as an expression of one of the
several difficulties of which we must be aware and for which
we must seek correctives.

Certainly, before selecting his subject, the psychobiographer should make sure that a reasonable amount of psychologically viable information is available. Whenever possible, such
data should be looked for in primary sources. To rely on
secondary sources is to invite the sort of error one finds in a
recent life, the author of which suggests that the strange behavior of one of the lesser characters in the story might be
traceable to statements in a letter written by the character's
mother during his early years. Had the author gone behind
the secondary works on which she depended for this speculation, she would have learned that the letter which so trauma-
tized the character in his childhood did not come to his attention until he was a man in his sixties.

Defenders of psychobiographical writing argue that as
between the psychotherapist and the psychobiographer, the
advantages tend to even out.

The psychotherapist, to be sure, has the patient before
him, but ordinarily for only a short time, whereas the psychobiographer has within his sights the whole life of his subject.

The therapist obtains the bulk of his information from
one person only—the patient. The psychobiographer, on the
other hand, can expand and modify the portrait of his subject
by quoting what the subject's contemporaries thought about

him. "For important public figures," Runyan reminds us, "confidential information about their lives (including material on their sexual experience, unusual family circumstances, or controversial aspects of their career) is sometimes not released or available until after their death and the death of immediate relatives."

If the patient is a creative person—writer, artist, composer—the therapist can examine only such imaginative works as exist at the time the patient consults him. On the other hand, the biographer, hunting for clues to the interior conflicts and mind-states of the subject, can draw on the entire body of his creative work.

The therapist can extract dream material from his patient. Although in the record open to the biographer this kind of matter is scanty, it is not nonexistent. Richard Wagner, in one of his letters, describes the dream that underlies several of his operas, a circumstance that his psychobiographer was delighted to discover. Emanuel Swedenborg regularly jotted down his dreams; and Virginia Woolf, two years before her death, recorded a dream that Edel utilizes to good effect in his *Bloomsbury.*

Fantasies, it must be admitted, are hard to come by. So is the evidence that only free association, one of the tools of the therapist, can produce. Still it is a mistake for the biographer to assume that such things are never obtainable.

Frank Manuel was able to make something of Isaac Newton's practice in his youth of listing words more or less alphabetically and more or less as they occurred to him. "In the Morgan notebook," writes Manuel, ". . . the word *Orphan* . . . precedes *Offender.*" This is indeed a suggestive coupling, for by the time of Isaac's birth his father was dead and two years later his mother, having remarried, went to live in the home of her new husband, leaving Isaac to be brought up by his maternal grandmother. In the Morgan notebook, Manuel notes, the word "Mother" is followed by a string of nouns ending with the word "Whore."

Surrogates for "free associations," Runyan points out, "have been found in the 'language exercises' of Heinrich Schliemann in which he revealed dreams and unconscious wishes," and one of Theodore Roosevelt's biographers analyzes caricatures drawn by Roosevelt as an adolescent, in which he pictures members of his family turning into animals.

Undeniably, some psychobiographies exhibit inadequate or faulty data, but the same can be said of some traditional biographies. Regardless of what kind of life you attempt, the rule to follow would seem to be Bernard Shaw's "Get your facts right first."

Missing Evidence

Another objection offered by the critics of psychobiographical writing has to do with the handling of gaps in the record. Your subject behaves in some incomprehensible manner, but when you review his life, searching for a damaging incident or relationship to explain his odd ways, you find little or nothing.

No matter what kind of life you're doing, this is a tough problem; and some commentators assert that the demands of psychobiography are such that it lends itself to the practice of filling gaps in the record with unfounded conjectures—conjectures that say to the reader in effect, "Because at age fifty-five John acted thus, it follows that at age five this or that wounding experience must have befallen him." Of this device Bernard De Voto opined years ago: "Biography proper is not concerned with the *must* but only with the *did*."

Even Runyan, no enemy of psychobiography as he himself broadly defines it, concedes that the practice of "retrodiction"—the assumption that a known action by the subject can be described as the result of an unprovable prior occurrence

—"is especially troubling when the earlier event is later assumed to have been firmly established." In the same passage, however, Runyan quotes with approval a persuasive defense of the use of retrodiction under certain circumstances as set forth by John Cody in his *After Great Pain: The Inner Life of Emily Dickinson.*

"Psychoanalysis," Cody says, "is not alone among sciences in providing a means whereby the existence of what is not directly perceptible can be inferred. Thus, the psychoanalytic interpretation of the life of a historical figure is in certain respects comparable to the reassembling of a fossil skeleton" by incorporation into the structure of one or more plastic bones. One such plastic bone in Cody's biography of Dickinson, according to its author, is "the assumption that in early life she experienced what she interpreted as a cruel rejection by her mother. Many of her statements, her choice of certain recurring metaphors and symbols [in her poems], and the entire course of her life, viewed psychoanalytically, argue for the truth of this assumption."

Obviously, there are conditions under which the use of an assumption, grounded on a combination of solid fact and plausible theory, is justified and desirable. Just as obviously, the manner in which the author presents these mixtures of fact and guess is the all-important factor.

For a skillful handling of a psychologically based conjecture, let's turn again to the biography of Sir Henry Clinton by William B. Willcox, a book already mentioned (see Chapter 9) in these pages.

When Willcox found it difficult to understand aspects of his subject's conduct, it will be recalled, he sought the assistance of Frederick Wyatt, an experienced psychotherapist. Working together, Willcox and Wyatt concluded that Sir Henry's often contradictory actions were the outgrowth of an unresolved childhood crisis—only to realize, in due time, that what little information they had about Sir Henry's early years yielded no incidents directly supportive of such a theory.

At this point Willcox confronted what can be called the biographer's dilemma: should he try to explain Sir Henry's adult behavior by postulating the existence of an unprovable childhood conflict? Unable to make his hero's actions comprehensible in any other way, Willcox boldly resolved to do so. And to us, as writers, the instructive thing is how he went about it.

"I have attempted, in fairness to the reader," he explains in the introduction to his *Portrait of a General: Sir Henry Clinton in the War of Independence,* "to keep from suggesting [the existence of a childhood trauma] . . . in the body of the narrative. My description of Sir Henry's career is doubtless colored by such understanding of his neurosis as Wyatt and I have obtained, but that understanding is necessarily tentative, like all historical theory; and the only time to advance it is after marshalling the evidence that it purports to explain. I have therefore described Clinton's conduct, pointed out its oddities, and left till the end the attempt to fit them into a coherent if unconscious behavioral pattern. The reader is thus free to examine the man and his career, and then accept or reject our theory of why the career was a failure."

In keeping with this plan, Willcox confines the discussion of his and Wyatt's theory to the twelfth and final chapter of *Portrait of a General*—and to make certain that the reader realizes that the author is speculating, he entitles the chapter "The General and the Man: An Interpretation."

Using Willcox's work as a textbook, let's fashion a couple of rules covering the use of psychological theory to bring out the meaning of documented actions:

> *make sure the reader knows you're guessing when you are,*
> *and*
> *refrain from treating such conjectures as though they were established*
> *fact.*

"No one," John A. Garraty writes in his wonderfully enlightening *The Nature of Biography,* "should object to the use of Freudian techniques if they are explicitly described as speculations and if known facts are not twisted or ignored in order to bring the subject into a preconceived pattern."

Unfairness

Another often-heard censure is that since many of the theories of psychoanalysis have been derived from a study of neurotics and psychotics, life portraits resting on such theories tend to overemphasize the negative aspects of their heroes and heroines. What does it profit us to be told why Vincent Van Gogh cut off his ear and gave it to a prostitute if the chronicler of the great Dutch painter's life fails to indicate the sources, inner and outer, responsible for his artistic brilliance and productivity?

Again we are in the presence of a legitimate criticism that, far from indicting psychobiographical writing, simply expresses another of the difficulties inherent in such work—a difficulty that we must try to overcome by thorough research, an examination of our own prejudices toward the subject, and a minimal use of technical terms.

Research

No human being is merely the sum of the inner determinants of his personality. Not to be neglected by his biographer are the equally important outer influences—social, political, religious, etc. "[A] biographical subject," Edel has remarked, "is not a patient and not in need of therapy." Biography readers yearn to meet the hero in his entirety, not the occasional invalid; and no self-respecting writer wants the smell of ether wafting from his pages.

Though psychological factors undergird Manuel's biography of Isaac Newton, one is impressed by the author's copious attention to the effect on the great scientist of the mores of his time and place and on the part played in the formation of Newton's character by a rigidly puritanical upbringing. Robert G. L. Waite has revealed that in assembling the material for his *The Psychopathic God: Adolf Hitler* he did not think of himself as compelled "to choose between clinical psychology on the one hand and . . . political history on the other." Instead, he utilized data from both fields, gathering information that allowed him to show how, from the time of the First Reich on, the development of Germany engendered a culture receptive to a man of Hitler's psychic makeup.

Prejudices

"Psycho-historians," Jacques Barzun has written, "see others moved by unconscious forces that distort vision and compel strange behavior, but they assume themselves to be clear transmitters of light and judgment. Why is their vision of persons and events not blurred and skewed as well, and their interpretation forced upon them by dark needs rather than evidential reasons?"

Barzun's astringent words are worth taking to heart. If you don't like your subject, it's easy—too easy—to put him or her down by recourse to pathologically oriented psychological concepts. To guard against this unfair strategy, you must not only recognize the nature and extent of your own hostilities but also seek to neutralize them by putting yourself in the subject's shoes; by trying to see and sense the world as he or she saw and sensed it—in short, by employing that detached but compassionate understanding of the subject that imparts such balance to Edel's five-volume biography of Henry James.

Technical Terms

Some writers, Edel and Manuel among them, take the position that the terms special to the various psychological disciplines should not be used at all in biographies directed to the general reader.

This would seem to be excellent advice.

For one thing, sophisticated psychological concepts are not readily grasped. How can you be certain that you understand the constructs on which you're relying until you can say them in your own words?

For another, technical terms constitute part of the raw material gathered by research. Like all such data, they should be processed by the mind of the writer and put into plain English before being passed on to the reader.

It's your book. Write it in your language.

Simplism

Still another often-vented stricture is that the authors of psychobiography sometimes reduce complex human beings to Johnny-One-Notes by tracing all their deeds and attitudes back to a single (usually childhood) event.

For this legitimate complaint there is but one remedy: don't do it. The biographer should bring to his labors a respect for the complexities of the human being, for what Tennyson called "the abysmal depths of personality."

CHAPTER 14

Handling Quotes

Few keys on the typewriter of the biographer undergo more use than the one bearing the inverted commas. The biographer is a quoting animal. He quotes from personal documents, from commentary on his characters by the characters' contemporaries, from secondary works consulted for corroborative details and background information, from remarks gathered in interviews, and from general literature. Sometimes even his title is a quote; or derives from one, as is true of Catherine Drinker Bowen's *Francis Bacon: The Temper of a Man,* inspired by Plutarch's assertion in his *Lives* that "Authority and place demonstrate and try the tempers of men by moving every passion and discovering every frailty."

Since as a biographer you must do considerable quoting, it's important that you familiarize yourself with those sections of the current (1976) Copyright Act dealing with "fair use" of copyrighted "works of authorship"; and you can obtain a copy of the Act free of charge from the Copyright Office, Library of Congress, Washington, D.C. 20559, or you can find it in a public library, if you want to consult the Act or copy it.

Works of authorship, according to the Act, include books, magazines, newspapers, motion pictures, plays, musicals, and a number of other things. If a work of authorship is not under copyright—Shakespeare's plays and poems, for example—it is regarded as being "in the public domain" and you can quote from it freely. Such is not the case, however, with copyrighted works. Under some circumstances you can take a small amount of material, a phrase or a few sentences, from a copyrighted work of authorship; but under other circumstances you cannot use such material unless you obtain written permission to do so from the holder of the copyright.

One thing every writer should understand is this: a work of authorship does not need to be published to come under the protection of the Copyright Act. In fact, unpublished works are candidates for little or no fair use. Herewith are a couple of examples:

Letters to the Author

Suppose you're gathering material for a life of a person still living or only recently dead. Naturally, you're going to seek information from people who know or knew the individual. Suppose you write one of these people, asking him to jot down and send to you his recollections of your subject. Suppose he does so.

Who owns this letter to you? All you own is the letter as a physical object. Ownership of its contents remains with the person who wrote the letter.

Hence the necessity, whenever you solicit information by mail, of requesting the right to reproduce the letter or its contents in your work.

Manuscripts of Work in Progress

Occasionally this kind of material comes into your hands. When it does, be careful how you use it. Again, let's hypothesize a for-instance.

For your biography you need data on, say, sailboats. It so happens that someone is writing a book on the subject and is kind enough to let you read a portion of his or her manuscript. If you wish to use material from this work in progress, you must obtain the written permission of its author. Generally, even information, put into your own words but taken directly from such a manuscript, can be used only if the author of the manuscript allows you to do so. At stake in this matter is a valuable thing—the right of an author to be the first to publish whatever he has written.

Copyright is a form of property. When you use material from a copyrighted work, published or otherwise, you are appropriating something that belongs to somebody else. As to under what circumstances you can quote freely as distinct from those circumstances under which you must seek permission—*there are no exact rules.* Every case must be considered separately, in the light of the following questions:

For what purpose are you using the quoted material: in a commercial book that you hope to sell to the general public, or in one connected with a non-profit educational undertaking? No one needs to be told that the courts may frown on the use of material for commercial intent and make allowances for its use for non-profit instructional purposes.

What is the nature of the copyrighted work from which you are taking the material? Many factors must be considered here. If you're taking largely factual material from the news columns of a newspaper, chances are it's safe to use quotes so long as they are of a reasonable length. If you're quoting from the editorials or the op-ed page, chances are you must get permission. Different magazines have different policies about quoting, and your best bet is to call the magazine and ascertain what its rules are. If you're quoting from an out-of-print book and the material is not unreasonably extensive, you may be safe. If you're quoting from an in-print book, watch out.

How much material are you quoting relative to the length of the copyrighted work as a whole? Nine times out of ten you are free to use a brief amount of material—a phrase or a few sentences; but it's worth noting that nowhere in the Copyright Act is there a definition of what "brief" is.

What effect is your use of the material likely to have on "the potential market for or value of the copyrighted book"? The authors of *The Rights of Authors and Artists,* an American Civil Liberties Union handbook, point out that the courts often consider this to be the most important factor. "As one put it," they write, "the central question in the determination of fair use is 'whether the infringing work *tends* to diminish or prejudice the potential sale of plaintiff's works.' "

When in doubt as to whether you should or should not seek permission, err on the side of prudence. Request the permission.

How do you do this?

Write the original publisher of the material. If he controls the copyright, he can grant permission; if not, he can usually tell you with whom to get in touch. If this request goes unanswered, send it a second time by registered mail, return receipt requested.

If the publisher does not know who controls the copyright, seek this information from the Search Division, Register of Copyrights, Washington, D.C. 20540. This can take a fair amount of time, so allow for this in your schedule. The Search Division charges a fee, depending on the length of the search. If it can't help you, find a substitute for the material.

Your permission request should provide the following information:

About your book to be—the work in which you wish to use the material:

Your name as author, the title of your book, your publisher, the approximate date of publication, the nature of the work (hardbound or paperback, trade or text edition), the approximate price and number of printed pages. Consult your editor about the kind of rights (e.g., non-exclusive world rights) to request.

About the source of the material you wish to use:

The author(s), title, date of publication, and page number or numbers of the work (book magazine, etc.) in which the material appears. Be sure to indicate exactly what material you wish to quote. This can be done in one of two ways: (1) by supplying the opening and closing words of the passage or passages to be used or (2) by enclosing a photocopy of enough of your manuscript to show the copyright holder the material you want.

And don't forget—most permissions carry fees, chargeable to you.

How the biographer handles quoted material—the panache with which he does it—affects the readability of his work; and the requirements of effective quoting can be examined in the light of a few suggestions.

Keep to a minimum direct quotes from letters.

Occasionally a letter is so crucial to the intent of your book that you have to use all or most of it. If the letter is short, it's usually best to put it between quote marks and to so merge it into the text that it does little or no damage to the consistency of tone that characterizes good writing. If it's long, you have no choice but to present it in blocks of indented or otherwise set-off matter sans quote marks.

When this becomes necessary, and especially when the letter runs on for more than a page, make certain the reader understands its importance. Otherwise he may skip it, for there's something about an extended mass of set-off print that repels—like the elevated freeways that segregate in more ways than the merely physical some of the neighborhoods of our towns and cities.

Few letters are worthy of being given in full. The most

effective way of treating nearly every letter is to paraphrase its contents, merging in a few direct quotes from it as you do so.

Bear in mind that no matter where a letter comes from —a correspondent or a collection of manuscripts—it does not belong to you and even a paraphrase of its contents may be an infringement of copyright.

Avoid repetitions.

Don't convey in your own words the information contained in whatever direct quotes you use. Don't, for example, paraphrase a letter and then present the letter itself. The paraphrase tells us what we need to know. So does the direct quote. But we don't need both.

Notice how Russell Baker sidesteps saying it twice in the following passage from a chapter of his *Growing Up* wherein he reproduces portions of the letters written to his mother by a man named Oluf:

> On April 14 he confided that he was $1000 in debt.
> "I talk to the Caschier [sic] in our Bank today, asking him to lett [sic] me have 1500 Dollars, he said, not now, but come in here middle of next month. I think then you can have it, ef [sic] I do I will come to you. . . . "

Make certain nothing in the quote confuses the reader.

Few things are more annoying than the presence in quoted material of references to persons, places, and events that are either unknown to the reader or irrelevant to the point the material is making. References of this sort can be handled in one or a combination of ways:

1. By using the ellipsis—the three dots indicating that something has been removed—to get rid of the confusing statements. Remember, of course, to use four dots whenever the omitted material ends a sentence.

In the first draft of a biography on which a friend of mine is working, he quoted this passage from a long letter:

> On what ground or pretext the Jury could have acted, I am utterly at a loss to conceive unless the call of two hours on Wilkinson which was made by my son on his descent to New Orleans was placed to my account, & deemed sufficient to enroll me with the party. He, it seems, saw & took tea with Mrs. Blennerhassett only, but I have never seen either the lady or her husband. So much for the charge treason.

On examining the first draft, my friend realized that since nowhere in the preceding section of the book had he identified either Mrs. Blennerhassett or her husband, the passing reference to them could only puzzle. In his second draft, therefore, he altered the quote to read:

> On what ground or pretext the Jury could have acted, I am utterly at a loss to conceive unless the call of two hours on Wilkinson which was made by my son on his descent to New Orleans was placed to my account, & deemed sufficient to enroll me with the party. . . . So much for the charge treason.

2. By inserting a bracketed explanation, as in the following quote from a diary:

> Mary took the trouble today to tell me [by a hand-delivered message, we learn from one of her letters] that she never wished to lay eyes on me again.

3. By so distributing the quoted matter as to permit the insertion of explanations and commentary in the writer's own words, as in this passage from Edel's *Bloomsbury:*

> Vanessa, said Virginia in later years, "has volcanoes underneath her sedate manner." This was true; but the volcanoes rarely erupted. The world saw a quiet, composed Vanessa, a woman of few words. "You have an atmosphere," her sister

told her. That atmosphere embodied her heritage of Cambridge integrity and her established role as the oldest child of Leslie and Julia. By the time she was briefly at the Slade School, Will Rothenstein found she had "the quiet courage of opinions." He added, a bit enigmatically, "She spoke with the voice of Gauguin." What are we to make of this? Gauguin's voice in his journals is harsh and edged with life's cruelties. We may judge Vanessa knew how to deliver a snub when she thought it necessary.

Whenever possible, melt the quote or quotes unobtrusively into the text.

The section from *Bloomsbury* just reproduced provides a good example of this procedure.

Whenever possible, convert into your own words what others have said or written about the persons in your story.

But remember, paraphrasing can be copyright infringement. Ideas *only* can be used. You must change more than merely the words—you must change their order and construction.

When research turns up picturesquely phrased descriptions of the personality or physical appearance of the individuals under study, one is always tempted to use them verbatim. More often than not the temptation should be resisted. If you incorporate more than brief quotes, you are taking for yourself the author's expression.

The rule underlying my suggestion to use quotes sparingly and unobtrusively has already been stated: it's your book; put all of it you possibly can into your own language.

Again and again the biographer finds himself looking for brief and pithy quotations—sometimes to fortify or justify a judgment he wishes to make, other times for the purpose of adding spice and color to his description of a person or place, or to his account of an event.

This being the case, it is a good idea to have on hand a few quotation-locating tools, such as *The Oxford Dictionary of Quotations, Bartlett's Familiar Quotations,* Arthur Richmond's *Modern Quotations,* and Ambrose Bierce's *The Devil's Dictionary.*

Every big dictionary is an excellent compendium of quotes, especially the *Oxford English Dictionary,* the etymologies of which teem with phrases and sentences showing the usage of the words. Say you wish to round off your comments on the effect of fame on your hero with something apt and aphoristic. In the *OED,* under the substantive form of the word, you'll find no less than fifty-one expressions containing it, among them these glistening odds and ends: "The desire of fame be that last weakness wise men put off," "Fame . . . that second life in others' breath," "In retirement he sighed for the fame-giving chair," "Fame is the thirst of youth," and "Athens . . . was more famous than fame-worthy."

Of course, in using quotations of this sort, the principles of fair use apply.

CHAPTER 15

Handling Notes and Bibliography

MANY biographies require documentation, the inclusion of notes showing from what manuscripts, books, articles, persons, or other sources the writer derived the authority for his remarks. Sometimes, too, the documenting of a work entails the preparation of a bibliography.

There's no universally accepted way for performing these tasks. If your publisher has style rules, follow them. If not, select a system suitable to your subject from either *The Chicago Manual of Style* or *The MLA Style Sheet*—and stick with it, for in documentation consistency is the rule. Low-priced paperbacks based on these widely used reference books are available. Kate L. Turabian's *A Manual for Writers of Term Papers, Theses, and Dissertations* digests the *Chicago Manual,* and Dean Memering's *Research Writing: A Complete Guide to Research Papers* does the same for the MLA work.

Writing notes and bibliographies is not difficult. If you're doing it for the first time, as has already been suggested, a comfortable procedure is to use one of the style manuals as a guide. After you've documented a manuscript or two in this fashion, you can shelve the manual—to be referred to, thereafter, only when problems arise. Arise they will. Indeed, every now and then you'll be forced to handle documentation for which no established form exists. In these instances, the rule to bear in mind is that when consistency and clarity clash, let consistency go to smash.

Since the style manuals detail all the accepted rules of citing, we can confine ourselves in these pages to those aspects of documentation of greatest interest to the biographer.

TYPES AND PURPOSES OF NOTES

Notes fall into three categories.

Reference Notes

As the term indicates, these show the sources to which you have gone for ideas and facts.

Explanation Notes

Also called content notes or discussion notes, these add something to the text by conveying diverting or informative material that, were it incorporated in the text itself, would confuse or distract the reader. In the opening chapter of *Peter the Great,* for example, Robert K. Massie describes the city of Moscow as it was in his hero's day.

> Across the square from Assumption Cathedral [he writes] stood the Cathedral of the Archangel Michael, where the tsars were entombed. . . . In the middle of the small room, three carved stone coffins held Ivan the Terrible and his two sons. . . . Tsar Alexis, father of Peter the Great, and two of his sons, also tsars, would lie in this same small room but they would be the last. Alexis' third son, Peter, would build a new cathedral in a new city on the Baltic where he and all the Romanovs who followed would be entombed.*

At this point the asterisk inserted above the line and after the period calls attention to a note in smaller type at the bottom of the page:

> *Except Peter II, whose body is in the Kremlin, and Nicholas II, the last tsar, whose body was destroyed in a pit outside Ekaterinburg in the Urals.

Obviously, Massie has resorted to an explanation note to avoid destroying the sense of "being there" that his opening chapter is designed to evoke. Explanation notes should be simple, direct, conversational in tone, and brief. If one runs long, consider converting it into an appendix. That way you can reduce the explanation note to a reference note:

> *See Appendix I.

Combination Notes

These result when explanatory material is incorporated in reference notes. Bear in mind that what you're writing is primarily a reference, and that the citations to the sources must come first. Coming up is a combination note taken from E. Wilder Spaulding's biography of George Clinton, the first governor of New York. First Spaulding lists the sources for something said in the text, then he offers information he did not wish to include in the text and tells us the sources of some of this added information:

> T. E. V. Smith, *The City of New York in 1789* (New York, 1889), 22, 23, 31; *Magazine of American History,* 1889, p. 185; New York City Directories. The Government House is of course not to be confused with Federal Hall which was the old City Hall on Wall Street converted by L'Enfant to serve the federal government. Clinton's account book in the State Library shows he paid Henry White £130 on April 16, 1790 for

the rent of the Queen Street house. See New York City Hall of Records, Liber III, pp. 4ff. for the sale of No. 67 Pearl Street in 1815 for the benefit of Clinton's heirs.

Properly written, reference notes serve two purposes. They identify the nature of the source cited and show where in the source the author found his evidence. Specifying the nature of the source is important because, as Jacques Barzun and Henry F. Graff point out in *The Modern Researcher,* "sources are weighed, not counted." A reader is likely to put more credence in a book than in a magazine article. Data gathered by interview may impress him less than that found in a manuscript. In this excerpt from a reference note, the nature of the cited source is clear:

Esther Burr's manuscript diary.

If an unpublished diary or autobiography carries a title framed by its author, put that in quotation marks, followed by the phrase "diary of" or "autobiography of so-and-so," and drop the word "manuscript" or its abbreviation "Ms." Many sources identify themselves, as in this reference:

Thomas Jefferson to J. P. G. Muhlenberg, 31 Jan. 1781.

The expression "Somebody to Somebody" defines the nature of the source sufficiently. The word "letter" is not necessary. In most notes, page numbers or dates suffice to indicate the portions of the source cited. For manuscript collections some writers provide further data, such as the number of the box or folder where the manuscript reposes. One always identifies the collection and its whereabouts, as in this note:

Carroll Wilson to Mr. and Mrs. Louis Wilson, 16 Sept. 1924 (Carroll Wilson Collection, Archives, Massachusetts Institute of Technology, box 2, folder 36).

In a writing classroom certain queries about documentation repeatedly arise:

Do popular biographies of living persons need reference notes? Such books tend to rest on anecdotes, newspaper stories, letters by or to or about the subject, and commentary from critics and admirers. If these and all other sources used are clearly identified in the text, little or no further annotation is necessary.

Should all biographies of historical figures be formally documented? Why not? Notes add a dimension to a biography, a warmth, a sense on the part of the reader of having had a chat with the author. Certainly most birth-to-death lives should be annotated. Other types of biography may not require it.

"My chapters," Catherine Drinker Bowen writes in her *Francis Bacon,* "are cast in biographical form, yet they are in essence essays or opinion, the expression of one person's thinking about Francis Bacon. To encumber such a book with scholarly apparatus seemed superfluous. Conversation, excerpts from letters, et cetera, are fully documented [internally, which is to say, in the text]. No alterations of the original texts have been made beyond deletions as indicated by ellipses or in footnotes."

This is fair enough, coming as it does from Bowen, with her well-earned reputation for thorough research and even-handed analysis. She at any rate has the courtesy to talk to us, to explain the omission.

What should and shouldn't be annotated? "[W]rite a note," Barzun and Graff tell us, "whenever you think an alert person might feel curiosity about the source of your remarks." References should be provided for major developments, quotes of more than passing length, facts previously unreported, intricate arguments, debatable evaluations, and most characterizations, especially when these constitute a synthesis from a variety of sources—in which case all the sources relied on should be named.

Well-known facts—that the Civil War began at Fort Sumter, for example—need no affidavits. To document trivia —that the distance between two places is X miles, for example —is to trivialize the documentation itself.

TYPES AND PURPOSES OF BIBLIOGRAPHY

A bibliography assumes a variety of forms. Most common is the list of sources, alphabetically arranged so as to make it easy for the reader to locate those he wishes to consult on his own.

Source lists can be comprehensive or limited. A comprehensive list shows all the sources cited in the book along with most of the other sources examined for background purposes. A limited one, usually called a "Selected Bibliography," shows only the sources cited or those plus others that the author considers important to an understanding of his subject.

Source lists can be single or multiple.

In *Bloomsbury,* Leon Edel deals with nine individuals. As seven were writers and two artists, he divides his bibliography into these sections:

"Bloomsbury Group Writings." Here, under the names of the seven writers, he lists the titles of their publications, presenting the names alphabetically and the titles chronologically.

"Bloomsbury." A select list of books about the Bloomsbury group.

"Related Works." A somewhat expanded list; and
"Bloomsbury Painters." A one-paragraph author's note calling attention to a couple of books about the artists and to notes
about their works in various exhibition catalogs.

The nature of Edel's subject dictated the division of the
Bloomsbury bibliography. For other books the nature of the
sources may dictate the arrangement, giving us bibliographies
divided into segments, carrying headings such as:

Manuscripts
Printed Sources
Newspapers
Secondary Books

Another way of revealing sources takes a form commonly
headed "Bibliographical Essay." Instead of listing his sources,
the user of this method discusses and to some extent evaluates
them. How the essay is arranged varies. One can discuss the
sources in connection with aspects of the hero's life—"The
Early Years," "The War Years," etc. Or one can take them
up on a chapter-by-chapter basis or in accordance with the
nature of the sources cited.

In the essay, as in the list, all sources mentioned should
be so identified that the reader can consult them himself,
either to check on the author's veracity or for purposes of
further reading. In an essay, however, there is no need to
invert the names of any of the authors. As all the essential
information about cited sources can be provided in the reference notes, bibliographies are not mandatory—although I suspect that many readers, like this one, are always glad to see
them.

PLACEMENT OF NOTES

Back in the days when publishing costs were relatively modest, notes often appeared at the bottoms of the text pages —hence the designation of them as "footnotes." Today, owing to the rising cost of adjusting page makeup to notes, most of them have become what are interchangeably labeled "endnotes" or "backnotes." Instead of being put at the bottoms of the text pages, they are printed *en masse* at the end (back) of the book, usually after the text or the appendices and in front of the bibliography.

From the *Chicago Manual* comes this prophetic observation: "Computer elements, both hardware and software, can now be programmed to cope adequately and expeditiously and economically with the scholar's predilection for notes at the bottoms of pages, but until such technology, today available to a few, has become . . . available to all publishers, the footnote method of documentation must be considered a difficult luxury."

Tomorrow, then, perhaps a return to footnotes. Today endnotes prevail, although most publishers are not averse to the presence of a few explanatory notes at the bottoms of the pages.

STANDARD TERMS AND ROMAN NUMERALS

Over the years, in the interests of saving space, scholars have developed a number of standard terms—many of them abbreviations—for use in notes and bibliographies.

Today we no longer employ some of these devices, namely *op. cit., loc. cit., infra, supra,* and *v.* or *vide.*

Op. cit. is the abbreviation of *Opera citato,* meaning "in the work recently cited." Its disappearance in recent years is commendable. Suppose that on the first page of the reference notes you cite:

Lloyd Lewis, *Sherman: Fighting Prophet* (New York: Harcourt, Brace, 1932), p. 45.

If at a much later point in the notes you cite the same book thus:

Lewis, op. cit., p. 189,

the reader, wondering to which of Lewis's several books you're referring, must flip back to the original citation. Rather than put him to this trouble, substitute for the *op. cit.* a shortened title, thus:

Lewis, *Sherman,* p. 189.

As for *infra* (below), *supra* (above) and *v.* or *vide* (see), most modern writers are using their English equivalents.

Both the *Chicago Manual* and the *MLA Style Sheet* (and their digests) contain complete lists of the standard terms, and though you'll not use some of them, you should learn them all for obvious reasons. Nobody is about to excise the *op. cit. 's, loc. cit.'s, supra's, infra's,* and *vide's* from the older books that you may be studying for research purposes.

For many years Roman numerals have designated the volumes of multivolume books and periodicals. This practice remains acceptable, but some modern writers prefer the Arabic numbers. The biographer-as-researcher, however, must be able to read the Roman numerals, and for those who feel shaky about this, here they are:

1. I	6. VI	11. XI	16. XVI
2. II	7. VII	12. XII	17. XVII
3. III	8. VIII	13. XIII	18. XVIII

4. IV	9. IX	14. XIV	19. XIX
5. V	10. X	15. XV	20. XX

30. XXX	80. LXXX	400. CD	900. CM
40. XL	90. XC	500. D	1,000. M
50. L	100. C	600. DC	2,000. MM
60. LX	200. CC	700. DCC	3,000. MMM
70. LXX	300. CCC	800. DCCC	4,000. MV̄
			5,000. V̄

Notice that when the smaller number comes first, it is read as a subtraction from the larger number: IV = 4. When the smaller number follows the larger, it is read as an addition: VI = 6. A large number like 1,985 is not read as 19 + 85 but as 1,000 + 900 + 80 + 5: MCMLXXXV.

Another reason for learning the meaning of all standard terms is to avoid the confusion that arises when they're incorrectly used. This is especially true of the term *ibid.*, the abbreviation of *ibidem,* meaning "in the same place."

Two practices govern the use of *ibid.*, or, if you prefer, its English equivalent, "same."

1. Always follow *ibid.* by a page number or by some other indication of what portion of the source you're citing, and

2. use *ibid.* only when the source cited is identical to the last source listed in the preceding note.

If note 16 reads:

16. Lewis, *Sherman,* p. 45; Jefferson to Muhlenberg, 31 Jan. 1781 (TJ Papers, LC)

and you wish to refer to Lewis, *Sherman* again in note 17, you must write:

17. Lewis, *Sherman,* p. 45,

but if note 16 reads:

16. Jefferson to Muhlenberg, 31 Jan. 1781 (TJ Papers, LC); Lewis, *Sherman,* p. 45,

then you can write:

17. Ibid., p. 45.

Another frequently used term—"ed."—has several meanings: "editor," "edition," or "edited by." Its plural—"eds."—means either "editors" or "editions."

Often found in both the documentation and the text is the term "sic," meaning "thus it is, mistake in the original." Although "sic" is Latin, it may be anglicized and, as it is not an abbreviation, it needs no period. In the midst of quoted or italicized material, put it in brackets:

"All that glistens [sic] is not gold."

But when it can be inserted after the quoted or italicized material, put it in parentheses:

"All that glitters is not golden" (sic).

Other frequently used abbreviations are: f., meaning "and on the following page," ff., meaning "and on the following pages," and *passim,* meaning "here and there, at intervals." Always precede these abbreviations with the numbers or descriptions that show what part of the work you're citing —as in

Malcolm Cowley, ed., *Writers at Work* (New York: Viking Press, 1959), p. 25f.
Cowley, *Writers at Work,* pp. 30ff.
Cowley, *Writers at Work,* pp. 12–31, *passim.*
Cowley, *Writers at Work,* Introd. [for Introduction], *passim.*

FRAMING NOTES AND BIBLIOGRAPHIC ENTRIES

Reference notes and bibliographic entries are framed differently, and the same is true of first and subsequent reference notes.

Reference Notes and Bibliographic Entries

For a book, the first reference note can read:

> Lloyd Lewis, *Sherman: Fighting Prophet* (New York: Harcourt, Brace, 1932), 127.

For the same book, the bibliographic entry can read:

> Lewis, Lloyd. *Sherman: Fighting Prophet.* New York: Harcourt, Brace, 1932.

The differences stand out. Since numbers identify the reference notes, there's no need to invert the names of the authors as must be done in an alphabetically arranged bibliography. In a reference note, the major elements are divided by commas. This makes it possible, when two or more sources are cited, to separate them by semicolons, thus:

> Russell Baker, *Growing Up* (New York: Congdon & Weed, 1982), p. 37; Julius Pratt, "Aaron Burr and the Historians," *New York History* 26 (October 1945): 23; and Thomas Jefferson to Dr. Benjamin Waterhouse, 21 Mar. 1803 (Jefferson Papers, Library of Congress, 22435).

In a bibliographic entry, the main elements can be divided by periods.

In a reference note, information as to where, by whom, and when the book was published is usually enclosed in parentheses. In a bibliographic entry, it stands free. A reference note for a book always indicates what part of it the author is citing. The bibliographic entry rarely gives such information. A subtitle may be omitted from a reference note, thus:

> Lloyd Lewis, *Sherman* (New York: Harcourt, Brace, 1932), p. 127.

But it should be given in the bibliography. Note that when the edition of a book is mentioned in the bibliography, it is treated as a separate element, thus:

> Downie, N. M. and R. W. Heath. *Basic Statistical Methods.* 2d ed. New York: Harper & Row, 1965.

If a book has three or fewer authors, put all their names in both the reference note and the bibliography, and in the bibliography invert only the first name listed:

> Field, Frank, Molly Meacher, and Chris Pond. *To Him Who Hath: A Study of Poverty and Taxation.* New York: Penguin Books, 1977.

In a reference to a book having more than three authors, list them all or list only the first author, followed by the abbreviation *et al.* (for *et alia*) or by its English equivalent, "and others." But in the bibliography, list all the authors.

For a signed magazine article, the reference note reads:

> Philip Shriver, "The Beaver Wars and the Destruction of the Erie Nation," *Timeline* 1 (December 1984–January 1985): 29.

For the same article, the bibliographic entry reads:

> Shriver, Philip R. "The Beaver Wars and the Destruction of the Erie Nation." *Timeline* 1 (December 1984–January 1985): 29–35.

For an unsigned magazine article, the reference note reads:

> "Byrd of West Virginia: Fiddler in the Senate," *Time,* Jan. 23, 1978, p. 113.

Don't use the word "anonymous" in such notes and entries. For the circumstances under which that word can be used, see a style manual. For magazine articles, as for books, commas divide the elements of the reference notes and periods those of the bibliographic entries. The only other difference, aside from the arrangement of the main author's name, is that the reference note for an article gives only the page number or numbers cited, whereas the bibliographic entry shows all the pages that the article occupies in the periodical.

Governing the citation to all printed material are two rules worth memorizing:

1. Titles of books, magazines, newspapers, and other serials—such as the *Proceedings* of historical societies—are always italicized, meaning of course that in the typescript the titles are underlined.

2. Parts of books, magazines, newspapers, and other serials are always put in quotation marks and not italicized.

For the correct forming of citations to unprinted material —such as manuscripts and information obtained by interview, observation, or correspondence—consult either the *Chicago Manual* or the *MLA Style Sheet*.

First and Subsequent Reference Notes

If the first reference to a book reads:

Lloyd Lewis, *Sherman: Fighting Prophet* (New York: Harcourt, Brace, 1932), p. 123,

all subsequent references to the same book can read:

Lewis, *Sherman*, p. 133.

If the first reference to a signed magazine article reads:

Philip R. Shriver, "The Beaver Wars and the Destruction of the Erie Nation," *Timeline* 1 (December 1984–January 1985): 24,

all subsequent references to the same article can read:

Shriver, "The Beaver Wars," *Timeline* 1 (December 1984–January 1985): 24.

If the first reference to an unsigned magazine article reads:

"Byrd of West Virginia: Fiddler in the Senate," *Time,* Jan. 23, 1978, p. 13,

a subsequent reference to the same article can read:

"Byrd of West Virginia," *Time,* 23 Jan. 1978, p. 15.

NUMBERING ENDNOTES

Most modern biographers key endnotes either (1) to superior numbers, or (2) to page numbers.

1. Superior Numbers

To use this system, take the following steps:

Put numbers above the lines of the text and corresponding numbers before the related endnotes.

In the text, sequence the numbers chapter by chapter, beginning each chapter with number 1.

In the list of endnotes, repeat both the number of each chapter and its title (see Figure 1). This makes it easier for the reader to locate the endnotes to which the numbers in the text apply, and, as Figure 1 shows, you can render life still pleasanter for the reader by placing at the top of each page of endnotes a running head showing the pages in the text wherein the corresponding superior numbers appear. Then if the reader wishes to see the endnote referred to by superior number 10 on page 191, he has only to turn to the page carrying the running head "Notes for Pages 190–192."

38

18   Russell Baker, *Growing Up,* p. 37
19   Thomas Jefferson to J. P. G. Muhlenberg, 31 Jan. 1781 (*Papers of Thomas Jefferson,* IV., ed. Julian P. Boyd, p. 487).
21   Baker, *Growing Up,* p. 47.

Chapter 2. College Years

1   Philip R. Shriver, "The Beaver Wars and the Destruction of the Erie Nation," *Timeline* 1 (December 1984–January 1985): 29.
2   Same, p. 31.
3   Jefferson to P. S. DuPont, 18 Jan. 1802 (Boyd, *Papers,* VIII, p. 127n.).
4   Malcolm Cowley, ed., "How Writers Write," Introd., *Writers at Work* (New York: Viking Press, 1959), p. 3.
5   "Horatio Alger," *DAB* (1872).
6   Anthony Burgess, rev. of *Running Dog,* by Don DeLillo, *Saturday Review,* Sept. 16, 1978, p. 38.
7   U.S. Cong., House, *Agreement with Univ. of Texas for Lyndon B. Johnson Archival Depository,* 89th Cong., 1st sess., H Rpt. 892 (Washington, D.C.: GPO, 1965), p. 3
8   Enrico Caruso, *The Best of Caruso,* RCA Victor, LM-6056, 1958.

Fig. 1. A Page of Endnotes Keyed to Superior Numbers

Superior note numbers always follow punctuation marks, except in the case of a dash. The *Chicago Manual* illustrates this rule by these examples:

> "This," George Templeton Strong wrote approvingly, "is what our translators can do."[1]
> (In an earlier book he had said quite the opposite.)[3]
> This was obvious in the Shotwell series[1]—and it must be remembered that Shotwell was a student of Robinson.

The ideal place for a superior number is at the close of a paragraph. Whenever a number must go into the paragraph, try to put it at the end of a clause or, better, a sentence. Superior numbers distract when placed between the subject and verb of a sentence or between other related words. Let's now put these suggestions in the form of an example. In Chapter 3 of Fawn Brodie's *Thomas Jefferson: An Intimate History* this passage appears:

> With his daughters there was in his letters this chronic wistful appeal: Love me—I need you—"Do it for the additional incitement of increasing the happiness of him who loves you infinitely. . . . Continue to love me with all the warmth with which you are beloved."[12]

In the endnotes for Chapter 3: "A Sense of Family," the corresponding reference reads:

> 12. Jefferson to Martha Jefferson, April 7, March 28, 1787, *Family Letters*, 36–37.

2. Page Numbers

If you use this system, no superior numbers are needed and the following steps can be taken:

Precede each endnote with a phrase or quote showing to exactly what material on the corresponding page of the text the note refers (see Figure 2).

151 *"Thunderous Silence":* Col. Barrett to author.
152 *"The new disorder of things":* George Atcheson, Jr., to Hornbeck, 4 Jul 28, HP, File "Atcheson, G."
154 *Handball championship: Sentinel,* 13 Apr 29.

6. "Vinegar Joe," 1929–35

155 *"Intense desire to get my hands":* Pogue, I, 251.
156 *"Move, shoot and communicate":* Gen. Timberman, interview with author.
156 *"Wicked memory.":* K. Marshall, 9.
157 *Infantry Journal:* Stilwell's articles: "Caterpillar or Scorpion," November-December 1932; "Annual Maneuvers at Benning," July-August 1933; "Counsel for the Defense," *Cavalry Journal,* March-April 1933.

Fig. 2. Endnotes Keyed to Page Numbers, from Tuchman's *Stilwell*

Submit your list of endnotes to the editor when you mail your manuscript, but do not put in the page numbers, as these cannot be inserted until the page proofs of the printed book are available.

SPACE-SAVERS

Question every note and bibliographic entry. Is it necessary?

There are several ways by which you can keep the documentation within reasonable bounds.

1. Adapt to your purposes the numbering system used by Manchester in his *American Caesar*.

In these notes [Manchester writes] works are generally cited by the author's name only; for full listings see the bibliography. If the note is citing an author with more than one work in the bibliography, a brief title for the work is also given in the note.

If you follow this system, then instead of writing:

Burke Davis, *The Billy Mitchell Affair* (New York, 1967), 165; Frank Raymond Kelly and Cornelius Ryan, *McArthur: Man of Action* (New York, 1950), 44,

you can write:

Davis, *Mitchell,* 165; Kelley and Ryan, 44.

2. For sources that you must cite frequently, devise abbreviations. List these at the top of the endnotes and use them consistently in the references. If your list of abbreviations contains these entries:

CW. Carroll Wilson
CWC. The Carroll Wilson Collection in the Archives of The Massachusetts Institute of Technology,

you can write:

> CW to Mr. and Mrs. Louis Wilson, 16 Sept. 1924 (CWC).

3. Bunch the notes whenever you can do so without causing confusion. Perhaps you find yourself making in one paragraph five statements derived from five different sources. Instead of inserting a superior number after each statement, put one number at the end of the paragraph and put all five citations in the correspondingly numbered endnote—taking care to sequence the citations in the same order that you presented the statements in the text. If your chapters are divided into sections, with extra space between them, you may find it feasible to confine all or most of the superior numbers to the ends of the sections and to sequence the correspondingly numbered citations accordingly.

4. Except in the case of special editions, the first reference to a book can be reduced to the minimal information needed to identify it—namely, the full name of the author or authors and the title. Tradition dictates the inclusion of where, by whom, and when the book was published, but none of this information is necessary. Nor is the use of the letter "p." (for "page") except when you must use two or more numbers in a row, as in this note:

> Albert Jeremiah Beveridge, *The Life of John Marshall,* 3 [the volume number], p. 34,

where the "p." is needed for the sake of clarity.

Whatever space-saving system you follow, be consistent.

TYPING THE DOCUMENTATION

Double-space all notes and bibliographic material. The editor needs the space between the lines to insert changes and instructions to the printer.

Indent every note and bibliographic entry and treat it as a paragraph. Avoid using the same number twice. If you must add information between, say, notes 15 and 16, don't run in a note 15a. Instead, put the added material either at the end of note 15 or at the beginning of note 16 and adjust the superior numbers or the page numbers accordingly.

Begin a list of endnotes on a separate sheet of paper, but treat them as part of the manuscript. If, for example, the text or the appendices end on manuscript page 361, start the endnotes on page 362.

Even if your reference or combination notes are to go at the bottoms of the text pages, type all of them on a separate sheaf of paper and number the pages N1, N2, etc.

The best way to handle the occasional explanation footnote is to melt it into the manuscript in this manner:

With Burr declared innocent, the district attorney saw fit to ask —and the court to grant—that the treason indictments against those of his associates who had been brought to Richmond be quashed.* To Be sure the misdemeanor indictments remained

*David Floyd, also among those indicted, was never brought to Richmond, arrangements having been made for him to be tried in Indiana Territory. He was the only member of the expedition to be convicted (see page 381).

in force, but as the subsequent trial of Burr on that count [etc.]

CHAPTER 16

Going to Market

Iᴛ takes talent to write a biography, but it takes genius to sell one.

Am I exaggerating? Given the complexity of book publishing today, I think not. Certainly it takes effort, and the biographer can be described as taking his first steps to market when he finds an appealing subject and writes the best book he can.

The experienced author knows what to do from that point on. The beginner must learn as best he can how to select the publisher to which the kind of biography he's done should be directed, how to correspond with editors, how to prepare and submit a manuscript, and how to live with or without an agent.

SELECTING A PUBLISHER

A good way to launch this process is to draft a hope list —a list of publishers who regularly issue biographies, who handle them well, and whose titles indicate that they are open to the type of life you've written.

For the serious and painstakingly researched biography, the most likely buyers are the commercial publishers of hardbound books and the university presses. For popular biographies, particularly those dealing with contemporary celebrities, the possibilities are broader, including as they do the commercial publishers of paperbound originals.

Commercial houses are those interested in making money by selling their products to a general audience. They're often spoken of as "trade houses" because of their practice of extending to book dealers and jobbers a long, deep, or trade discount. A university press is one associated in some way with an institution of higher education. Add to these categories a large number of independent presses (a market the beginner should not overlook) and a number of regional presses (some of which are open to lives of local persons)—and you have a map of that section of today's publishing world of most interest to the biographer.

The subject you've selected may determine some of the entries on your hope list. A publisher specializing in scientific books for the general reader, for example, may welcome the life of a scientist. Lives of artists and other eminentos of the art world appear in the catalogs of publishers primarily interested in the critical and instructive aspects of the graphic arts.

To make certain of putting the right names on your list, study the current edition of *The Publisher's Trade List Annual.* This is a collection of publishers' catalogs, arranged alphabetically and bound in a series of volumes. Accessible at most libraries, it shows the in-print titles of practically all American trade houses and university presses, along with those of some of the more active small and regional presses. Mention has already been made of the importance, before selecting a subject, of checking out the one you're thinking of in the *Subject Guide to Books in Print* by way of ascertaining what your competition is, if any. An examination of this reference work will also help you determine what publishers are looking for biographical material.

The next step is to check out the names on your list in the current *Writer's Market*. This annual describes the requirements of 800-plus publishers, and further information of this sort is obtainable in *The International Directory of Little Magazines and Small Presses.*

Finally, check your list against the *Literary Market Place.* This is the directory of American book publishing. When the time comes to make your first submission, you'll need the name, address, and telephone number of the editor to whom your material is to be sent. LMP provides this information together with many other facts important to the market-bound writer.

When your list is ready, the data you've jotted down after each entry should include a note showing how that publisher wants you to submit material. *Writer's Market* and *The International Directory of Little Magazines and Small Presses* are the most convenient sources of these preferences.

If a publisher's capitulation of his requirements includes the word "Query," don't send your manuscript. Send a letter.

If it contains this sentence, "Query or submit outline/synopsis," or this, "Query with outline and sample chapters," accompany your letter with the items requested.

If it says, "We prefer full manuscript submission," mail the manuscript.

If it says, "No unsolicited queries or mss," assume that the publisher is considering only material submitted by agents or recommended by an established author or other person whose judgment the publisher trusts. If you have access to either, make the most of it; if not, simply leave that publisher off the hope list, consoling yourself with the thought that his loss is another publisher's gain.

A good query letter—one that gives a clear picture of what you've written and excites interest in it—merits a place among the higher art forms. Labor over yours. If it takes a day to compose, two days, longer—so be it. Remember that your career as a writer is on the line with every line you write.

It's not easy to bring off a query. You've just finished a long and difficult book. You've poured yourself into it and perhaps a hunk of the mortgage money too. You're tempted to call it a work of genius, a masterpiece. Hold the thought. It has been said that writing is the exercise of certain skills and virtues, and to the author on his way to market, the indispensable virtues are confidence and perseverance. Make clear to the editor that you believe in what you've written, but don't brag about it. Take comfort in the conviction that when your work reaches his desk the manuscript will do the bragging for you.

What goes into a query letter depends on the method of submission. If the publisher's instruction reads "Query" and nothing more, assume he means what he says. All he wants is a letter in which you describe what you've written and ask if he'd like to see either the manuscript or sample chapters and an outline.

As to the contents of a query, there are no formulae. The suggestion of matters to include, given below, is to be regarded as a checklist only. Some of the items proposed must be attended to in any query for obvious reasons. Others are optional. Still others call for information you may not be able to supply, and if there's a golden rule of query-writing, it's this: never tell an editor that you haven't done something. If you haven't published previously, say nothing whatsoever about it. If fifteen other publishers have turned you down, that's nobody else's business.

Now for some of the things that must go into a query, along with some you may wish to add:

    1. As early in the letter as possible, make the following

clear: the type of book you're offering, whether your subject is alive or dead, what his or her major significance is or was, what his or her dates are, and the title you've given the work. All of which could be taken care of in this opening sentence:

> I have just completed a biography of Christopher Columbus (1451?–1506), the discoverer of America. I call it *Rediscovering Columbus.*

Be sure to include a possible title. That way you and the editor have a convenient handle for use in future correspondence. If I were an editor, I'd be disturbed at the absence of a title in a query, wondering to myself: Does the author's failure to mention one mean that his thoughts on this subject have not yet crystallized?

2. If your hero has been the subject of previous books, show how yours differs:

> Another work, you may wonder, on the Admiral of the Ocean Sea? To that understandable concern my answer is this; all of Columbus's major biographers have treated him as a man ahead of his times, a precursor of today's scientifically oriented explorers. But my examination of the available original and secondary material on the Italian-born mariner who called himself "Christoferens" (the bearer of Christ) has convinced me that this was not the case. Columbus was wholly a man of his place and time—neither ahead of them nor behind—and the motives that sent him four times across a dangerous and hitherto little-traveled sea were not scientific but religious.

3. If you've learned something new about your subject —something unknown to either his contemporaries or to history—stress this matter and describe briefly the evidence on which your discovery rests.

4. If there are no previously published lives of your per-

son, make sure the editor understands why he or she deserves biographical attention.

5. Include some personal information, especially those aspects of your career that define your qualifications for dealing with the subject of the book. If your hero is an explorer, the editor may find it of interest that you've done some exploring.

6. Suggest possible audiences for the work. If your subject is a religious figure, remind the editor that the United States has some 4,000 religious bookstores, 1,500 secular bookstores with large religious departments, and 1,500 religious libraries. If your subject is clearly of interest to academia, mention the existence of 3,000 college bookstores with nine million student buyers and 1,700 college libraries. Most editors are aware in a general way of the library possibilities of a biography, but if you know of certain literary- or history-oriented institutions interested in your hero or heroine, so inform the editor. Do the same if you've reason to believe that your subject will appeal to the members of some national or international organization—to a society set up to promote country music, for example, or the American Bar Association.

Familiarity with the magazine of the book industry, *Publishers Weekly,* can be helpful in ascertaining the nature and size of potential audiences.

7. If you have a publishing record, describe it. If this information is impressive, supply it as early in the letter as possible and enclose whatever supporting evidence—clippings of reviews, sales figures, and the like—you can assemble.

8. Try to include, in quotation marks, a few sentences from your manuscript, thus providing a measure of your qualities as a stylist. If possible, infuse a flash of humor, a quip that the editor can dine out on next week. If you're not good at

this sort of thing, don't try. Businesslike is better than the *bon mot* that bombs.

9. If you possess relevant art work, describe it—but unless your book is built around such matter, don't send material of this sort until the editor requests it.

10. Like most letters, a query is typed single-spaced with double-spacing between the paragraphs.

So much for the full-scale query.

If you're submitting to a publisher who wants an outline and sample chapters, you can restrict the query to an abbreviated presentation of the essentials:

> type of book
> its title
> time and place and significance of the subject
> how your biography differs from previous ones, if any
> your publishing record, if any (if none, skip this item)
> personal data indicative of your expertise with regard to the
>   subject of the book

Strictly speaking, this kind of query is a cover letter. Its principal purpose is to call attention to the items enclosed, namely:

> a table of contents
> an outline of the book
> sample material from the manuscript
> pertinent clippings—and, incidentally, send no impertinent
>   ones. The editor is unlikely to be interested in a copy of the
>   prize-winning theme you wrote in college, unless it dealt in
>   a professional way with the subject of your present book.

Write the outline in the present tense. For most projects your best bet is to put it in the form of an expanded table of contents, showing under each chapter heading the developments therein and the order in which they are presented—as in this example:

Chapter 1.
Island Boyhood

Alexander Hamilton's remark in mid-life (that there "are strong minds that will rise superior to the disadvantages of situation") viewed as reflecting his memories of a troubled boyhood on the islands of Nevis and St. Croix in the West Indies—his mother a product of a broken home—her unhappy marriage—her flight from it, to live for fifteen years, unwedded, with Alexander's father—birth of Alexander's brother—his character—birth of Alexander in Charlestown, chief city of Nevis: date unknown but believed to be 11 Jan. 1752—physical appearance and commercial and agricultural pursuits of Nevis and Charlestown—Alexander's first brush with the existence of black slavery—his attitude toward it, as deduced from his subsequent battles against it—his father's noble background —his character—his career on Nevis—movement of family to Christiansted on St. Croix—disappearance of the father and speculations as to the why of Alexander's continuing affection for him—his mother's struggles to support Alexander and his brother—Alexander's education—his longing to distinguish himself, especially on the battlefield—his interest in war a life-long passion—how his description in a newspaper of the hurricane of August 1772 brings his skills as a penman to the attention of Rev. Alexander Knox and other islanders, who pool their resources to send Alexander to Great Britain's American colonies to continue his education and seek his fortune.

Submit sample chapters in sequence, beginning with Chapter 1. On occasion, circumstances may justify a deviation from this practice. If you're submitting three chapters, you may wish to send Chapters 1 and 2 along with whatever subsequent chapter best illuminates the major theme of the book. If you've written an introduction, include it, especially if it summarizes the biography and discusses your major sources of information.

As all writers know, any unsolicited material mailed to an editor—queries and queries with outlines and sample items included—must be accompanied by an SASE (a self-addressed, stamped envelope). As it's impractical to send an SASE with a boxed manuscript, clip to the enclosed cover letter enough postage for the return of the material.

PREPARATION AND SUBMISSION OF A MANUSCRIPT

One of my childhood memories is of a woman whom my mother brought in for her semi-annual wars on accumulated dust and disarray. The young lady was always stylishly attired, and her first act on arrival was to change into the old clothes she'd brought along. "As my grandmother used to say," she told me one morning, "you can't work pretty."

No biographer does. He labors in an escalating chaos of wandering notes and misplaced books. Endless revisions macerate his mounting manuscript into near unreadability. Even what he hopes is the final draft is for the most part a hodgepodge of interlineations, of lines snaking up and down the margins, of "see over's" to remind himself of inserts scratched on the backs of the sheets.

When the time comes to go to market, he must replace the old garments in which he has clothed his prose with something akin to a Chanel gown or a Brooks suit.

What should it look like, this typescript that is to bear your words—and hopes—to the eyes of an editor?

To begin with, all of the text and all of the front-of-the-book and back-of-the-book matter are double-spaced. This means bibliographies, notes, quoted passages, tables, captions —everything! Indent paragraphs uniformly, five spaces each.

Leave at least a one-inch margin at the bottom and sides of every page. Number the manuscript pages consecutively at the upper right-hand corner.

Before you start typing, clean the keys to avoid look-alike e's, o's, u's, n's, and a's.

Forgo fancy type of any sort—use only pica or elite. If your machine boasts a font of italics, forget it. *Underline* the words you want the printer to italicize.

Use a black and reasonably new ribbon and white paper, 8½ by 11 inches in size. What's called 20-pound bond is good. Never use an "erasable" or "corrasable" bond. You can tell this by its greasy feel. A lot is going to be written on your manuscript before it reaches the printer, and you don't want it to smudge.

Need I tell you to type on one side of the paper only?

If your chapters are divided into sections, signify the breaks between them in one of two ways. If you're using neither numbers nor subheads, drop down two spaces from the last line of a section and center the symbol # on the page. Then drop down two more spaces and begin the succeeding section. If you're using either a number or a subhead, put that at the center instead of the #.

There's no need for a title page, although no editor is going to reject your book if, like this writer, you prefer to use one. If you do, center the title of the book in the middle of the page and put all of it in capital letters. Drop down two spaces and center the word "by" in lower-case. Drop down two more spaces and center your name or pen name in upper-lower-case. Where you place the other requisite information—name, address, and telephone number—is immaterial, but it's well to avoid the upper-left-hand corner, as editors are prone to clip notes to manuscript pages in that quadrant.

If you don't use a cover page, put your name, address, etc., in the upper-right-hand corner of an unnumbered first page and center the title of the book and your byline a little above the middle of the page, thus:

ALEXANDER HAMILTON:
THE NATIONAL ADVENTURE, 1788–1804
by Broadus Mitchell

Then, if you're using an introduction, drop down four spaces and center the word INTRODUCTION or its equivalent in all caps, and then drop down four more spaces and begin the text. If you're not using an introduction, center the number and title of the opening chapter, thus:

Chapter 1
ISLAND BOYHOOD

Begin every succeeding chapter or other major division of the book at the same point—just above the middle of its opening page.

Some publishers have so-called "spec sheets," showing how they want a manuscript typed. If the one you're interested in does, send for it, enclosing an SASE.

Once your submission copy is ready, scrutinize it. If you can persuade someone else to read it too, do so. Watch for typos and misspellings, for inadvertent lapses of grammar. This is no time to do a revision, on a large or small scale. Before your opus reaches the typewriter it should be free of contradictions and illogicalities, of sentences that fail to say what you intended, of transitions that, instead of luring the reader on, stop him by calling attention to themselves.

Granted you've done this, you may find you still must make some marks on the typescript. Whenever possible, type in corrections—always in the space above, drawing a firm line through the word or words to be replaced and using a caret (∧) to indicate where the new word or words go. If typing in the new stuff proves difficult, print it in, shaping the letters with care.

Don't use a pen to correct the manuscript. Use a pencil with a sharp black lead. Then, if at the last minute you decide to put something back the way it was, you can erase the marks. If, however, you fear the erasure will muddy the copy, put dots under the words to be kept and the annotation "stet" in the margin. "Stet" is a Latin word meaning "Let it stand." It's one of the more useful of the standard proofreaders' marks. But don't feel you have to use proofreaders' marks in making final typescript corrections. They were created for marking tightly set proof pages. And as for marking the manuscript for the typesetter, that's the copy editor's job.

If you feel that any of your corrections might puzzle the editor, put an explanatory note in the margin of the manuscript. Such notes are useful for calling attention to deliberately misspelled or misused words, unusual constructions such as Greek letters and accents, and other special symbols.

If you find yourself making one or more large changes or four or more small ones on a page, retype the page. If such changes increase the wordage so that the material no longer fits the page, use an extra sheet. Number it "a" (e.g., "126 a"). If you're inserting a big chunk of material, continue the letter system ("126 b," "126 c," etc.). There's no point in renumbering the entire manuscript to accommodate new material.

When the opposite happens—when you end up with a partly filled page—follow one of two procedures. If the last line ends a paragraph, put no marks on the page. The editor will understand. If the last line does not end a paragraph, indicate that this is the case by penciling a straight line from the end of the last word to the bottom right-hand corner of the page.

Should you end up with nothing on a page, keep the

numbering system intact by following this procedure: if now you have no wordage for, say, page 77, renumber page 76 to read 76–77.

If these guidelines for typing a clear and correct manuscript seem beyond your skills, hire a professional typist to do the job.

Before mailing the manuscript, make sure the carbon or photocopy you retain reflects all the changes made in it.

Don't bind, staple together, or otherwise confine the pages of the manuscript. They're to be worked on and therefore must be mailed loose.

MULTIPLE SUBMISSIONS

Time was when sending a manuscript or a query to more than one publisher at a time was a mortal sin. Times change. Today simultaneous or multiple submissions are not unheard of. Some old-line publishers don't like the practice, but more and more publishers are beginning to concede that after a writer has spent from a year to an infinity on a book, he should not have to endure the delays of sequential submission.

Give this matter thought. What about the two or three publishers at the top of your hope list? If you know they're averse to simultaneous submission, send the material to them one after the other. If this effort produces no buyer, consider multiple submission for the remainder of the list. But be sure to say in your covering letter that you've sent the proposal to several other houses.

Once a manuscript is in the mail, try to put it out of your mind for the time being. Do something else; start another book. If three or four months pass and you receive no word, don't take to the phone. Send the editor a reminder letter. Tell him or her when the material was submitted and what it was, and ask when you may expect a report on it. This should bring a reply in a few weeks. If it doesn't, try one or two more such letters. If they're ignored, send a registered letter (return receipt requested), asking the editor to return the material and informing him that you're submitting it elsewhere. That a copy of your manuscript remains in his hands is of no consequence. Under the current copyright law, protection of your book begins with its creation. No one can publish it until you (and your collaborators, if any) grant him the right to do so.

Brace yourself for rejections. They hurt, yes, but they're part of the writing business: honorable wounds that eventually heal. Don't try to read anything into a rejection. No matter how politely it is worded, it means what it says. What it says to *you* is this: send the manuscript to someone else. Too commonplace for repetition are the horror stories of the many publishers who passed up a best-seller and the glory story of the one who saw its value.

Again—in dealing with a publisher you do not know, stay off the phone. Stick to the mails.

LIVING WITH OR WITHOUT AN AGENT

"An agent," Dwight Swain writes in his *Techniques of the Selling Writer,* "is a business manager for writers.

"If you have a business to manage . . . an agent can be invaluable to you. If you haven't, why should he waste his time?"

If you're doing your first biography, if you have no publishing record or only a run-of-the-mill one behind you, your time is precious too.

Don't waste it looking for an agent. Good ones are elusive. Bad ones—fly-by-nights and pseudos—won't do you a bit of good.

Concentrate on what you're doing. Complete the book. Prepare a typescript that shines. Labor over a query letter. Get the manuscript into the mail—and keep it there.

"Who knows?" as Rex Stout said long ago. "Some damn-fool editor may buy it."

Suggested Reading

I. RELEVANT TO BIOGRAPHICAL WRITING

Allport, Gordon W. *The Use of Personal Documents in Psychological Science.* New York: Social Science Research Council, 1942.

Anderson, James William. "The Methodology of Psychological Biography." *Journal of Interdisciplinary History* 2 (Winter 1981): 455–75.

Anderson, Terry H. "Becoming Sane with Psychobiography." *The Historian* 41 (1978): 1–20.

The Association of American University Presses. *Directory 1982–1983.* New York: American University Press Services.

Barzun, Jacques, and Henry F. Graff. *The Modern Researcher.* Rev. ed. New York: Harcourt, Brace & World, 1970.

Biography. A quarterly published in Honolulu by the University Press of Hawaii for the Biographical Research Center.

Bowen, Catherine Drinker. *Adventures of a Biographer.* Boston: Little, Brown, 1959.

———. *Biography: The Craft and the Calling.* Boston: Little, Brown, 1969.

———. "The Magnificence of Age." *Harper's,* April 1953.

Bradford, Gamaliel. *Biography and the Human Heart.* Essay Index Reprint Series. Freeport, N.Y.: Books for Libraries Press, 1969.

———. *The Journal of Gamaliel Bradford, 1883–1932.* Ed. Van Wyck Brooks. Boston: Houghton Mifflin, 1933.

Brady, John. *The Craft of Interviewing.* Cincinnati: Writers' Digest Books, 1976.

Brande, Dorothea. *Becoming a Writer.* Reprint of the 1934 ed. published by Harcourt, Brace. Los Angeles: J. P. Tarcher, 1981.

Broder, D. P. "The Adjective-Verb Quotient: A Contribution to the Psychology of Language." *Psychological Record,* III (1940), 310–430.

Brownstone, David M., and Irene M. Franck. *The Dictionary of Publishing.* New York: Van Nostrand Reinhold, 1982.

Burr, Anna Robeson. *The Autobiography: A Critical and Comparative Study.* Boston: Houghton Mifflin, 1909.

Butler, Lord. *The Difficult Art of Autobiography.* The Romanes Lecture Delivered in the Sheldonian Theatre 22 Nov. 1967. Oxford at the Clarendon Press, 1968.

The Chicago Manual of Style. 13th ed., rev. & expanded. Chicago: University of Chicago Press, 1982.

Clarke, Gerald. "Biography Comes of Age." *Time,* July 2, 1979.

Cockshut, A. O. J. *The Art of Autobiography in 19th and 20th Century England.* New Haven: Yale University Press, 1985.

Coe, Richard N. *When the Grass Was Taller: Autobiography and the Experience of Childhood.* New Haven: Yale University Press, 1984.

Dewey, John. *Art as Experience.* New York: Capricorn Books, 1959.

Dictionary of Behavioral Science. Compiled and ed. by Benjamin B. Wolman. New York: Van Nostrand Reinhold, 1973.

Directory: Historical Societies and Agencies in the United States and Canada. 12th ed. Compiled and edited by Tracey Linton Craig. Nashville, Tenn.: American Association for State and Local History, [1982].

Dixon, Janice T., and Dora D. Flack. *Preserving Your Past.* Garden City, N.Y.: Doubleday, 1977.

Dollard, John and O. H. Mowrer. "A Method of Measuring Tension in Personal Documents." *Journal of Abnormal and Social Psychology* 42 (1947): 3–32.

Dooley, Lucille. "Psychoanalytic Studies of Genius." *American Journal of Psychology,* 27 (1916): 263–416. Summaries of several early psychobiographies.

Edel, Leon. *The Age of the Archive.* Middletown, Conn.: Wesleyan University Press, 1966.

————. *Literary Biography.* Bloomington: Indiana University Press, 1959.

————. *Writing Lives.* New York: Norton, 1984, 1959.

Garraty, John A. *The Nature of Biography.* 1st Vintage ed., New York: Knopf and Random House, 1964.

Gibaldi, Joseph, and Walter S. Achtert. *MLA Handbook for Writers of Research Papers, Theses and Dissertations.* Student Edition. New York: Modern Language Association, 1980.

Guide to Reference Books. Edited by Eugene Paul Sheey. Chicago: American Library Association, 1976.

Hook, Sidney. *The Hero in History.* Boston: Beacon, 1943, 1935.

The International Directory of Little Magazines and Small Presses. Ed. Les Fulton and Ellen Berber. 19th ed., 1983–84. Paradise, Calif.; Dustbooks.

Kendall, Paul Murray. *The Art of Biography.* New York: Crown, 1978.

MacCampbell, Donald. *The Writing Business.* New York: Crown, 1978.

Mallon, Thomas. *A Book of One's Own: People and Their Diaries.* New York: Ticknor & Fields, 1984.

Mathieu, Aron. *The Book Market: How to Write, Publish and Market Your Book.* New York: Andover Press, 1981.

The MLA Style Sheet. Ed. William R. Parker. Rev. ed. New York: Modern Language Association, 1967.

New Directions in Biography. Essays by Phyllis Auty, Leon Edel, Michael Holroyd, Noel C. Manganyi, Gabriele Merle, Margot Peters, and Shouchi Saeki. Ed. and with foreword by Anthony M. Friedson. Honolulu: Published for the Biographical Research Center by the University Press of Hawaii, 1979.

Norwick, Kenneth P., and Jerry Simon Chasen, with Henry R.

Kaufman. *The Rights of Authors and Artists: The Basic ACLU Guide to the Legal Rights of Authors and Artists.* An American Civil Liberties Union Handbook. New York: Bantam, 1984.

Passler, David. *Time, Form, and Style in Boswell's Life of Johnson.* New Haven: Yale University Press, 1971.

Provost, Gary. "A Basic Guide to Selling Your Words." *Writer's Digest,* November 1982, pp. 24–29.

The Publishers' Trade List Annual. New York: Bowker, 1984.

Runyan, William McKinley. *Life Histories and Psychobiography: Explorations in Theory and Method.* New York: Oxford University Press, 1982.

———. "Why Did Van Gogh Cut Off His Ear? The Problem of Alternative Explanations in Psychobiography." *Journal of Personality and Social Psychology* 40 (1981): 1070–77.

Smith, Bradford. "Biographers' Creed." *William & Mary Quarterly* 3rd Series, No. 10 (1953): 180–85.

Strunk, William, Jr., and E. B. White. *The Elements of Style.* New York: Macmillan, 1959.

Swain, Dwight V. *Techniques of the Selling Writer.* Norman: University of Oklahoma Press, 1965, 1973.

Taylor, Mark. "The Appetite for Lives." *Commonweal,* Jan. 18, 1980.

Telling Lives: The Biographer's Art. Ed. Marc Pachter. Washington, D.C.: New Republic Books, 1979.

Tolles, Frederick B. "The Biographer's Craft." *South Atlantic Quarterly,* 53 (1954), 508–520.

Tuchman, Barbara W. *Practicing History.* New York: Knopf, 1981.

Turabian, Kate L. *A Manual for Writers of Term Papers, Theses, and Dissertations.* 4th ed. Chicago: University of Chicago Press, 1973.

Vice, Giambattista. *The Autobiography.* Trans. with an introd. by Max Harold Fisch and Thomas Goddard Bergin. Ithaca, N.Y.: Cornell University Press, 1944.

White, Ralph K. "Black Boy: A Value Analysis." *Journal of Abnormal and Social Psychology,* 62 (1947), 440–461.

Winks, Robin, ed. *The Historian as Detective: Essays on Evidence.* New York: Harper & Row, 1968.

Winslow, Donald J. *Life-Writing.* Honolulu: Published for the Biographical Research Center by the University Press of Hawaii, 1980.

Woolf, Virginia. "The Art of Biography." *Atlantic Monthly* 163 (1959), 506–510.

——. *Granite and Rainbow.* Part II: "The Art of Biography." New York: Harcourt, Brace, 1958.

World Guide to Libraries. 5th ed. Detroit: Gale Research Co., 1980.

Writer's Market. Cincinnati: Writer's Digest Books, 1985.

Yelton, Donald Charles. *Brief American Lives.* Metuchen, N.J.: Scarecrow Press, 1978.

Zinsser, William. *On Writing Well: An Informal Guide to Writing Nonfiction.* New York: Harper & Row, 1976.

II. BIOGRAPHIES AND AUTOBIOGRAPHIES CITED IN THIS BOOK

St. Augustine. *Confessions.* Franklin Center, Penn: Franklin Library, 1980.

Baker, Lewis. *The Percys of Mississippi: Politics and Literature in the New South.* Southern Biography Series. Baton Rouge: Louisiana State University Press, 1983.

Baker, Russell. *Growing Up.* New York: Congdon & Weed, 1982.

Bashkirtseff, Marie. *Journal of a Young Artist.* Paris: Mazarine, 1980.

Bate, Walter Jackson. *Samuel Johnson.* New York: Harcourt Brace Jovanovich, 1977.

Bowen, Catherine Drinker. *Francis Bacon: The Temper of a Man.* Boston: Little, Brown, 1963.

——. *Yankee from Olympus.* Boston: Little, Brown, 1944.

Bowers, Claude G. *Jefferson and Hamilton.* Boston: Houghton Mifflin, 1925.

Bradford, Gamaliel. Sketch of Henry Clay in *As God Made Them.* Port Washington, N.Y.: Kennikat Press, 1969.

Brittain, Vera. *Testament of Youth.* Originally published in Great Britain by Victor Gollancz Ltd., 1933. Published in U.S.A. by Seaview Books, 1980.

Brodie, Fawn M. *Thomas Jefferson: An Intimate History.* New York: Norton, 1974.

Caesar, Gaius Julius. *Commentaries of Caesar Translated into English.* 2 vols. New York: AMS Press, [1979].

Carroll, Peter N. *The Other Samuel Johnson: A Psychohistory of Early New England.* Cranbury, N.J.: Fairleigh Dickinson University Press, 1978.

Chateaubriand. *Mémoires d'Outre-tombe.* Paris: Larousse, 1973.

Chute, Marchette. *Shakespeare of London.* New York: Dutton, 1949.

Cody, John. *After Great Pain: The Inner Life of Emily Dickinson.* Cambridge, Mass.: Harvard University Press, 1971.

Cumberland, William H. *Wallace M. Short: Iowa Rebel.* Replica Edition. Ames: Iowa State University Press, 1983.

Donald, David. *Charles Sumner and the Coming of the Civil War.* New York: Knopf, 1960.

Edel, Leon. *Bloomsbury: A House of Lions.* New York: Lippincott & Crowell, 1979.

————. *Henry James.* 5 vols. Philadelphia: Lippincott, 1953–1972.

Flexner, James. *George Washington* . . . 4 vols. Boston: Little, Brown, 1965–1972.

Franklin, Benjamin. *The Autobiography of Benjamin Franklin.* Illustrated Modern Library ed. New York: Barnes, 1944.

Freud, Sigmund. *Leonardo da Vinci.* New York: Moffat, Yard, 1916.

Godbold, E. Stanly, Jr., and Robert H. Woody. *Christopher Gadsden and the American Revolution.* Knoxville: University of Tennessee Press, 1982.

Grant, Dorothy F. *John England: American Christopher.* Milwaukee: Bruce, 1949.

Guedalla, Philip. *Wellington.* New York: Harper & Brothers, 1931.

Heilbroner, Robert L. *The Worldly Philosophers.* 3d. ed., rev. New York: Simon and Schuster, 1969.

Hindle, Brooks. *David Rittenhouse.* New York: Arno Press, 1980.

Holroyd, Michael. *Lytton Strachey: A Critical Biography.* New York: Holt, Rinehart and Winston, 1968.

Hughes, Rupert. *George Washington.* 3 vols. New York: Morrow, 1926–30.

James, Marquis. *The Life of Andrew Jackson.* Indianapolis and New York: Bobbs-Merrill, 1938.

Jenkins, Elizabeth. *Elizabeth the Great.* New York: Coward-McCann, 1959.

Karlen, Arno. *Napoleon's Glands and Other Ventures in Biohistory.* Boston: Little, Brown, 1984.

Kazin, Alfred. *New York Jew.* New York: Knopf, 1978.

———. *Starting Out in the Thirties.* Boston: Little, Brown, 1965.

———. *A Walker in the City.* New York: Harcourt, Brace, 1951.

Lash, Joseph P. *Love, Eleanor: Eleanor Roosevelt and Her Friends.* New York: Doubleday, 1982.

Levinson, Robert E. *The Jews in the California Gold Rush.* New York: KTAV Publishing House, 1978.

Lewis, Lloyd. *Sherman: Fighting Prophet.* New York: Harcourt, Brace, 1932.

Lomask, Milton. *Aaron Burr: The Conspiracy and Years of Exile, 1805–1836.* New York: Farrar, Straus & Giroux, 1982.

———. *Aaron Burr: The Years from Princeton to Vice President, 1756–1805.* New York: Farrar, Straus & Giroux, 1979.

———. *Andrew Johnson: President on Trial.* New York: Farrar, Straus & Giroux, 1960.

Lowell, James Russell. Sketch of Thoreau in *My Study Windows.* Boston: J. R. Osgood, 1871.

Ludwig, Emil. *Napoleon.* New York: Boni & Liveright, 1926.

Macalpine, I., and R. Hunter. *George III and the Mad Business.* New York: Pantheon, 1969.

Malcolm X. *The Autobiography of Malcolm X.* New York: Grove, 1965.

Manchester, William. *American Caesar: Douglas MacArthur 1880–1964.* New York: Dell, 1978.

Manuel, Frank E. *A Portrait of Isaac Newton.* Cambridge, Mass.: Harvard University Press, 1968.

Markham, Felix. *Napoleon.* New York: New American Library, 1963.

Massie, Robert K. *Peter the Great: His Life and World.* New York: Knopf, 1980.

Maury, William M. *Alexander "Boss" Shepherd and the Board of Public Works.* Washington, D.C.: George Washington University Studies, No. 3, 1978.

Milford, Nancy. *Zelda: A Biography.* New York: Harper & Row, 1970.

Morison, Samuel Eliot. *Admiral of the Ocean Sea.* Boston: Little, Brown, 1942.

Nagel, Paul C. *Descent from Glory: Four Generations of the John Adams Family.* New York: Oxford University Press, 1983.

Newman, John Henry. *Apologia pro Vita Sua.* New York: Norton, 1968.

Nicholson, Irene. *Liberators.* New York: Praeger, 1969.

Plutarch. *Plutarch's "Lives."* New York: Biblo and Tannen, 1966.

Prescott, Hilda. *A Spanish Tudor: The Life of Bloody Mary.* New York: AMS Press, 1970. Repr. of 1940 ed.

Rousseau, Jean Jacques. *The Confessions of Jean Jacques Rousseau.* New York: Modern Library, 1945.

Sainte-Beuve, C. A. *Portraits of the Seventeenth Century.* With an introd. by Ruth Mulhauser. Trans. Katherine P. Wormley. 2 vols. New York: Frederick Ungar, 1964.

Schorer, Mark. *Sinclair Lewis: An American Life.* New York: McGraw-Hill, 1961.

Spaulding, E. Wilder. *His Excellency George Clinton: Critic of the Constitution.* 2d ed. Port Washington, N.Y.: Ira J. Friedman, 1964.

Strachey, Lytton. *Elizabeth and Essex.* New York: Harcourt, Brace, 1928

———. *Eminent Victorians.* New York: Harcourt, Brace, 1918.

———. *Queen Victoria.* New York: Harcourt, Brace, 1921.

Swanberg, W. A. *Citizen Hearst.* New York: Scribner's, 1961.

———. *Luce and His Empire.* New York: Scribner's, 1972.

Tuchman, Barbara W. *Stilwell and the American Experience in China, 1911–45* New York: Macmillan, 1971.

Waite, Robert G. L. *The Psychopathic God.* New York: Basic Books, 1977.

Willcox, William B. *Portrait of a General: Sir Henry Clinton in the War of Independence.* New York: Knopf, 1962.

Wolff, Geoffrey. *Black Sun.* New York: Random House, 1974.

Yeats, William Butler. *Autobiography: Consisting of Reveries Over Childhood and Youth.* New York: Macmillan, 1944.

Index